Guide to
Motor Insurers' Bureau Claims

Guide to
Motor Insurers' Bureau
Claims

Donald B Williams
BA, LLB, Solicitor

This edition published in Great Britain 2000 by Blackstone Press Limited, Aldine Place, London W12 8AA. Telephone (020) 8740 2277 www.blackstonepress.com

© Donald B Williams, 1999

Seventh edition, 1999
Eighth edition, 2000

ISBN: 1 84174 124 8

Originally published in 1969 by Oyez Publishing under the title
The Motor Insurers' Bureau

British Library Cataloguing in Publication Data
A CIP catalogue record for this book is available from the British Library

Typeset by Montage Studios Ltd, Horsmonden, Kent
Printed by Ashford Colour Press, Gosport, Hants

Contents

Preface

The Motor Insurers' Bureau has, over the years since its inception in 1946, increased in importance in its role as provider of compensation for those injured in road traffic accidents for whom redress is not otherwise available. The chief functions of the Bureau relate to claims which would otherwise have been pursued against the 'hit and run' driver and the uninsured driver. The range of circumstances for which the Bureau provides has increased as the risks compulsorily insurable by motorists have widened. The Bureau now covers damage to property in addition to personal injury claims relating to uninsured motorists. Such damage became compulsorily insurable from 31 December 1988, following an EC Directive. A further EC Directive (90/232), which is concerned with certain aspects of Guarantee Fund activity, was adopted on 14 May 1990. Although it required implementation by 31 December 1992, effect had been given in the UK to its requirements by means of informal arrangements not requiring a further Agreement.

The initial impetus for writing this short guide in the first place arose out of my professional involvement in the 1964 case of *Adams* v *Andrews*, which helped to bring about changes in the MIB's arrangements. It was also my purpose to give publicity to the fact that claims can be made on the Bureau in cases which might otherwise seem incapable of redress. Many lawyers are still not as aware and some not fully aware of the victim's right to bring a claim on the Bureau.

My Scottish colleagues will no doubt share my pleasure, at long last, that the new 'Uninsured Drivers Agreement' recognises the differing terms and effects of Scots law.

This book is intended as an easily assimilible outline of the scope and workings of the Bureau; it is intended for lawyers as well as insurance companies and legal advice centres.

I would like to thank Mr James A Read, Chief Executive of the Bureau, and Mr Roger Snook, its Claims Manager, for all the invaluable assistance they have given me in connection with this edition.

Donald B Williams
January 2000

One

Introduction

1. Gaps in the law

By the time the 'roaring twenties' in the twentieth century had come to a close, horseless vehicles had already roared past the stage of development which rendered them capable of being extremely dangerous. It was against this background that the Road Traffic Act 1930 came into being. Indeed, one purpose of the Act, as stated in the Preamble, was 'to make provision for . . . protection of third parties against risks arising out of the use of motor vehicles'. Even though it may not have been fully realised at the time, it soon became apparent that there were certain types of risk for which there was no protection either under the Act or at all.

Thus, the 1930 Act gave no redress when a claim, rightly brought by someone who had suffered as a result of a motorist's negligent driving on the road, could not be, or otherwise was not, met, for some good reason, by the motorist or his or her insurers. Among this class of case were those in which the motorist at fault became, or was already, without means.

Some claims failed because a second or third motorist would drive off after a 'cutting-in' manoeuvre, leaving behind injured victims and damaged cars. The victim(s) would not normally have any information capable of leading to the discovery of the identity of the driver concerned and would thus not be in a position to bring proceedings.

Other examples arose out of incomplete insurance cover, for instance where the policy covered the motorist only for accidents arising in the course of his or her trade, and the particular accident occurred while the vehicle was being driven for social purposes (or vice versa).

Yet another illustration would be when the motorist had persuaded his or her insurers to provide a policy on the basis of some false statement or omission in the answers on the proposal form, thus negating the cover.

One could, of course, add to these examples. The more important types of case will be dealt with in greater detail later.

2.   The Cassel Committee

In brief, while the Road Traffic Act 1930 made insurance against third party claims compulsory, there was no provision in the Act, or elsewhere, for third parties to be compensated where the motorist had been negligent and was not covered, for some reason or another, by a policy of insurance. Arising from this situation a committee to consider compulsory insurance was set up under the chairmanship of Sir Felix Cassel KC. It comprised lawyers as well as insurers. The Report of the *Committee on Compulsory Insurance* came out in July 1937, and contained the following conclusions:

(a)   Where a claim was established against an uninsured motorist by a third party, the third party should have the right to recover from a central fund.

(b)   Where a motorist was unable to meet a claim brought by a third party, the same right should be available.

(c)   Where, however, a negligent motorist could not be traced (the 'hit and run' type of case), it was not feasible to extend a right to recover against a central fund.

(d)   Provision should be made for a solvency test of insurance companies to be administered by the Board of Trade, which would have power to grant or withhold a licence to carry on business as an insurer, and for a fund to be set up as a 'second line of defence' to meet claims due to be paid by insurance companies which became insolvent.

3.   The establishment of the Motor Insurers' Bureau

With a view to implementing *some* of the conclusions reached by the Cassel Committee, what has been described as 'an entirely novel piece of extra-statutory machinery' was set up with the co-operation of the major insurers. On 31 December 1945, the Minister of War Transport and the companies and Lloyd's syndicates dealing with motor insurance in this country entered into an agreement. Provision was made in that agreement for the establishment of a fund to be administered by a body to be set up. That body is now known as the Motor Insurers' Bureau.

The main object of the agreement was to implement the recommendation of the Cassel Committee to provide for compensation of victims of accidents occurring on the road where no compensation was available, or recoverable, due to the absence, or non-effectiveness, of insurance cover of the driver to blame for the accident. The agreement did not seek to fill any other of the 'gaps' outlined.

The Motor Insurers' Bureau is a company incorporated under the Companies Act 1929. Pursuant to an undertaking given by representatives of the companies dealing with motor insurance in this country, the parties to the original Motor Insurers' Bureau Agreement were the Ministry of Transport and the Bureau, whose liability under the initial agreement dates from 1 July 1946. The 1946 Agreement was supplemented by the 1969 Agreement, which applied only to 'hit and run' accidents occurring between 1 May 1969 and 30 November 1972.

There followed another Agreement, made between the Secretary of State for the Environment and the Bureau, which covered claims arising out of accidents caused by uninsured drivers only, and occurring on or after 1 March 1971.

Further Agreements related to accidents which occurred on or after 1 December 1972. They provided a remedy for claims arising out of accidents caused by uninsured as well as by untraced drivers.

A Directive of the European Communities on Motor Insurance in January 1984 required member states to extend third party insurance to include damage to property. A further agreement was therefore entered into in December 1988. That Agreement came into force on 31 December 1988 and applies to all claims arising out of accidents involving *uninsured* driver cases. It does *not* apply to unidentified ('hit and run') driver claims, as the Directive does not require these to be covered. The 1972 Agreement relating to untraced drivers remains in force. Similar but separate Agreements apply to Northern Ireland, the Channel Islands and the Isle of Man.

The current Agreement relating to uninsured drivers' claims is dated 13 August 1999 and applies to claims arising from accidents occurring on or after 1 October 1999.

The present address of the Bureau is 152 Silbury Boulevard, Central Milton Keynes, Milton Keynes, MK9 1NB, and communications are

usually addressed to the Secretary, a full-time official employed by the
Bureau. The present officers are Mr J A Read, Chief Executive; Mr R
Snook, Claims Manager; and Mr C B Garwood, Administration Manager
and Secretary. The telephone number is: 01908 240000, fax: 0908
671660, DX: 84753 Mk3.

4. Procedure for claiming

It should be borne in mind that the Bureau is not a court of law or tribunal.
However, it prefers to have claims submitted on forms it provides. The
forms are designed to produce the full range of necessary evidence in
support of the claim. Such evidence must, however, be presented in the
form required. Additional information may be required by the Bureau
(although not in the nature of an order of a court or tribunal for further
and better particulars). See p. 92 for an example of the form normally
used.

Complaints may be dealt with by telephoning the Bureau or its
appointed agent. Contact may be made by a Claimant in person or
through his solicitor or representative. If the complaint is not resolved by
speaking to the person handling the application, a letter may be sent,
setting out the basis for the complaint, to the Bureau's agent, marking the
envelope (and the letter) 'For the *personal* attention of the Claims
Manager'. If there is still no satisfactory resolution with the Bureau's
agent, a letter should be addressed to the Claims Manager at the Bureau.
The Chief Executive of the Bureau, Mr James A Read is always prepared
to review decisions taken on complaints. A letter should be addressed to
him for his personal attention. If the problem raises a matter of principle
which may be of public interest, after it has already gone through the
steps outlined above, a letter may be sent to the Minister for Roads and
Traffic at the Department of Transport, Enviroment and the Regions,
2 Marsham Street, London SW1P 3EB.

Two

Uninsured Driver Claims

1. Introduction

In cases where the offending motorist is not insured, the victim of an accident may still bring proceedings to recover damages for personal injuries. Since 1946, when the first Motor Insurers' Bureau Agreement came into operation, the Bureau has paid to a successful Claimant any sums due under the judgment, including costs, where the judgment is unsatisfied within seven days.

Under the 1988 Agreement, the Bureau's liabilities are extended to damage to property (principally vehicles, but also damage caused by colliding into a house, for example, or knocking over a bus stop), but with a maximum, currently fixed at £250,000 and with a minimum, currently £300. There are, however, a number of conditions to be met. These are examined in this chapter.

2. The uninsured driver

A man is knocked down by a car and is injured. The driver of the car ought to have been insured under the Road Traffic Acts against liability for this type of accident. The driver is not so insured. He happens to be a 'man of straw', making it pointless to seek compensation from him personally.

This was the first problem tackled by the Motor Insurers' Bureau. Clause 5 of the current Motor Insurers' Bureau Agreement, relating to uninsured drivers, covers this type of case. These provisions are to the effect that, if the victim successfully brings proceedings against the uninsured driver, the Bureau will pay the amount of the judgment and the costs awarded.

3.   What the Bureau will pay

Subject to the exceptions set out below, the Bureau will pay any amount outstanding under a judgment obtained by a victim claiming against an uninsured driver. The payment will include fixed, taxed or assessed costs. It will also include interest on the judgment debt (i.e., statutory interest which varies, at present 8 per cent).

If the claim includes a sum for items outside the Bureau's liability, the amount of the costs will be reduced by the appropriate proportion.

4.   The exceptions

(a)   Damage to property of £300 or less (that being the current 'excess' under the Agreement). In addition, any claim for such damages of an amount of more than £250,000 (that being the current maximum under the Agreement). (Clause 16(2)(3) and (4).)

(b)   Where there is no liability to insure (under Part VI of the Road Traffic Act 1988). An example would be where the vehicle was not being used on a 'road' within the definition laid down by s. 192 of the Act. (Clause 6(1)(b).)

(c)   Claims against the Crown (e.g., Government departments, armed forces) unless someone else has undertaken responsibility for motor insurance, or if the vehicle is in fact insured. (Clause 6(1)(a).)

(d)   A 'subrogated' claim, i.e., one made for the benefit of another person, e.g., arising under credit hire agreements. (Clause 6(1)(c).)

(e)   Any claim arising when the use was not covered by insurance, e.g., insurance with no business use cover but only domestic cover, and the Claimant knew or ought to have known that to be the case. (Clause 6(1)(d).)

(f)   Any claim (where the use was not covered) by a passenger who knew or could be taken to have known that the vehicle was uninsured, or had been stolen or used for crime. (Clause 6(1)(e), (2), (3) & (4).) This would cover the facts in the case of *Stinton* v *Stinton* (1995) RTR 157 (C of A). See p. 50.

(g)   Any claim relating to an accident caused by a hit-and-run (untraced) driver (see pp. 16–21).

(h)   Any claim where the Claimant has not assigned to the Bureau or its nominee the unsatisfied judgment, including costs and also not undertaken to repay the Bureau any sums paid to him under a judgment that has been set aside, and any sums received from other sources under the judgment. In other words, the Claimant must not benefit from a duplication of his damages claim. (Clause 15.)

5.   Burden of proof

The burden of proving that the Claimant knew or ought to have known of the absence or inadequacy of insurance cover, of any use in furtherance of crime (e.g. use of the vehicle as a 'getaway car') or that it had been stolen, is on the Bureau. However, it may accept as proof of the Claimant's knowledge, in the absence of any contrary evidence, his actual knowledge of any of the following:

(a)   That he himself was the owner or registered keeper or had caused or permitted its use.

(b)   That the driver was under age or disqualified under Licensing Law at the time.

(c)   That the user was not the owner or registered keeper or the employee of the owner or registered keeper or the owner or registered keeper of any other vehicle.

Included in the concept of the knowledge of the Claimant is any knowledge he could reasonably be expected to have had he not been under the self-induced influence of drink or drugs (clause 6(3)).

Thus had the circumstances in the case of *Stinton* v *Stinton* (see p. 50) arisen after 1 October 1999, there would probably have been no necessity for the litigation as the Bureau would have been in a position to rely on the facts as proof of the Claimant's knowledge of the driver (his brother) being uninsured.

'Knowledge' cases cause much difficulty (often resulting in litigation). *White* v *White and Motor Insurers' Bureau*, currently on its way from the Court of Appeal's judgment on 30 September 1998 is a case in point.

6.   Capacity of claimant

Where a solicitor or other representative of a Claimant is involved, any decision or act done to or by such representative or payment to him is treated as if done to, or by, or paid to, a Claimant of full age and capacity (clause 3). It seems that this clause has been inserted to protect the Bureau from claims it has had in the past of 'rogue' representatives who have not accounted fully (or, in some cases, at all) to the Claimant.

7.   Steps to be taken before issue of proceedings

It is for the Claimant to make reasonable enquiries to establish the existence of insurance cover of the vehicle causing the injury or damage. He must exercise the right under s. 154 of the Road Traffic Act 1988, i.e., to obtain relevant particulars of the insurance cover even if this involves him in expense. He must, therefore, make a formal complaint to the police if the demand for particulars is not complied with (and obtain from the police confirmation that he has done so — by obtaining a complaint number). All reasonable efforts have to be made to obtain that name and address of the registered keeper of the vehicle. The Claimant may be required to authorise the Bureau to make further enquiries on his behalf, presumably at the expense of the Bureau.

In other words, the Claimant is obliged to exchange names, addresses and insurance particulars with any others involved, to correspond with the owner or driver of the other vehicle, or his representatives. His own insurers require him to notify them of his claim. He is also obliged to make enquiries of the Driver and Vehicle Licencing Agency in Swansea (SA99 1BP) with a view to ascertaining the identity of the owner or driver.

If there are ascertained insurers, any claim must be directed to them even though the policy may not cover the relevant liability.

Where, as a result of enquiries, there is no insurance cover or if the insurer cannot be identified, or if the insurers contend that they are not obliged to deal with the claim, or for any other reason the insurers will not meet any judgment, the claim must be directed to the Bureau.

The application form is normally signed by the Claimant or his solicitor. The current Agreement gives the Bureau the right to refuse to accept the application — which will have the effect of its incurring no liability under the Agreement — if the form is signed by someone other than the Claimant or his solicitor. This will only be invoked if the Bureau is not satisfied as to the status of the party signing the form and his relationship with the Claimant and that the Claimant is fully aware of the contents and effect of the application (clause 7(2)).

It must be inferred from the introduction of this provision that some representatives not subject to lawyers' professional or other restraints have been troublesome in the past in pursuing claims on behalf of claimants without acting in their best interests and conducting the claims in a manner that would not be tolerated by the Bureau in dealing with Solicitors (or by the Law Society!).

8. Steps before proceedings leading to judgment

It should be noted that the Bureau may intervene even before a Claimant has obtained a judgment. It is thus open to a Claimant to apply to the Bureau *before* issuing proceedings against the uninsured driver.

Wherever possible, a claim should be made on the Bureau's application form along with supporting documents. The forms are available on request by post, telephone, fax or DX to the Bureau. The Claimant must also supply such further information and documents as may reasonably be required by the Bureau.

9. The 'time' element

The claimant must not, later than 14 days *after* issuing of proceedings, give notice to any identified insurer or to the Bureau, if no insurer has been identified. The notice must be accompanied by a copy of the claim form or other document originating the proceedings (in England and Wales) and, in addition, in proceedings in Scotland, a statement of the means of service (clause 9(1)(b)).

10. Further documents

Other documents required by the Bureau are:

(a) Copy, or details, of any insurance cover providing benefits for the Claimant (i.e., usually the Claimant's own, or his employer's policy).

(b) Copies of all correspondence between the Claimant (or solicitor or authorised agent) and the Defendant (or, in Scotland, Defender) or his solicitor, insurers or agent relating to the claim for which the Defendant (or Defender) may be covered.

(c) A copy of the particulars of claim whether or not indorsed on the claim form or other document originating the proceedings, whether or not served.

(d) A copy of all documents required under the Rules of Procedure to be served with the claim (e.g., medical reports and particulars of special damages). Updated medical reports must also be copied and sent to the Bureau.

(e)   the Bureau may require such reasonable further information to be supplied within a reasonable time as the condition of being liable under the Agreement (clause 11(2)). Any dispute arising out of the reasonableness or otherwise of such a requirement may be referred to the Secretary of State whose decision is final (clause 19). It is doubtful whether this will be applied other than on rare occasions. However, it provides some form of safety net in appropriate circumstances.

It is important to remember that it is for the Claimant to make sure that the notice and documents have been received by the Bureau by post or fax. The Bureau prefers service by fax as this can be proved by production of the claimant's fax record. Service by DX is *not* acceptable as delivery cannot be proved.

11.   Further steps required by the Bureau

The Bureau may require a Claimant to bring proceedings and take all reasonable steps to judgment against a party the Bureau contends to be responsible (wholly or partly) for the loss or damage. The Bureau will indemnify the Claimant as to the cost of such proceedings (clause 14(a)).

12.   Service of proceedings

(a)   A Claimant must notify the Bureau of the date of service of proceedings (in England or Wales) (clauses 10(1) and (2)).

(b)   Where the Court serves the claim form, notice must be given within *seven* days of receipt of notification of service by the Court or process server or after the date of actual personal service (presumably by solicitor).

In cases where service is 'deemed' to have occurred under the Civil Procedure Rules (i.e., where the Court serves on an individual or a limited liability company by first class post when it is 'deemed' to have been served two days after posting when it has not been returned to the Court) notice must be given fourteen days thereafter. It has been known for some Courts to delay sending notification of service, due to staff shortages or absences, computer breakdown or other reasons. Although in the notes to the Uninsured Drivers Agreement it is suggested that Claimants 'take steps to ensure that the Court or the Defendant's legal representatives inform them of the date of service as soon as possible', it is difficult to see how this may be effected. Perhaps a 'B/F' (i.e., 'Bring Forward') entry in one's diary or a computer programme would act as a reminder at an appropriate time or times for the busy practitioner to telephone, write or fax to find out if service has been effected, and when.

In Scotland the difficulty does not arise as notice would already have been given. There, very sensibly, proceedings are started at the date of service. (See *Miller* v *NCB* (1960) SC 376.)

13. Further steps before judgment

The Bureau must be kept informed of the progress of the proceedings. It may be useful for a solicitor to regard the Bureau *as if* it was in the position of an intelligent client who requires to be kept fully informed of all steps taken.

Thus filing a defence, amendment of particulars of claim and further (updating) medical reports, and the case being set down for hearing requires notification to the Bureau within seven days, with a copy of the relevant documents (clause 11(1)).

In cases where the Claimant wishes to take steps to sign or apply for judgment (i.e., in default of defence or summary judgment) notice must be given to the Bureau. This must be done at least thirty-five days *before* making the application, or the date when judgment is to be signed (clause 12).

If at any stage the MIB wishes to be joined as a party to the proceedings, the Claimant must not oppose such application. He must consent to such an order if requested. This provision is invoked in cases where there is a conflict between the Defendant (or Defender) and the Bureau, which can only be resolved by the Bureau becoming a Defendant or, in Scotland, a party minuter, if a Defence is to be filed on its behalf (see Note 7.4 to the current Agreement). This does not mean that the Bureau will be 'joined' in all cases. It is understood that the Bureau will, on receipt of a claim, state its intention to resolve matters by negotiation but that, if those representing the Claimant feel it necessary to issue proceedings, they will phone the Bureau to discuss whether or not the Bureau should be joined. This is in accordance with the practice of co-operation between the Bureau and solicitors and other representatives in attempting to achieve the objects of the various Agreements that apply.

14.   The position after judgment

Although the Bureau is obliged to make payment under a judgment not satisfied within seven days, such judgment may be set aside (or appealed successfully) and with it the Bureau's obligation to pay. The Bureau must notify a Claimant as soon as possible if it decides not to satisfy a judgment. Where a judgment is set aside, the Claimant is required to repay any sums received under it from the Bureau (clause 15(b)).

The Bureau is only obliged to make payment under a judgment if the Claimant has assigned any benefit he may have to the Bureau or its nominee (clause 15(a)).

There will be an apportionment of the sums recovered between the items for which the Bureau is and is not liable (clause 21).

Where there is difficulty in ascertaining whether the owner or driver of a vehicle has been correctly identified, the prudent Claimant (or prudent solicitor acting on his behalf) is advised to make sure that a claim is registered with the Bureau under the Untraced Drivers, as well as the Uninsured Drivers, Agreements. It is then for the Bureau to decide under which Agreement the claim will fall to be dealt with.

15.   The reasoned response

Under clause 18 of the current Agreement, the Bureau is under an obligation to provide a reasoned reply as soon as reasonably practicable to requests made regarding compensation payments (and presumably for refusing a compensation payment).

16.   Payment by the Bureau

If only part of the judgment debt is recoverable under the Bureau's scheme (for example, where a judgment in respect of damage to property exceeds the Bureau's financial limit, currently £250,000), the Bureau will pay to the successful plaintiff that part, which may also include the costs taxed pursuant to the judgment. Until recently the Bureau did not normally pay interest on the judgment debt or further costs, but there seems to be no legal basis for this practice. The Bureau had taken the view that interest payable on a judgment debt and any post-judgment costs do not form part of the judgment. The Bureau had, however, met claims for interest *included* in the judgment debt under the Law Reform (Miscellaneous Provisions) Act 1934 as amended by the Administration of Justice Act 1969.

It should be noted that there is nothing in the Agreement which affects the position at law of the parties to an action for damages arising out of the driving of a motor vehicle. The Claimant must successfully establish his case against the person (or persons, if more than one) responsible for the accident in the usual way and must recover judgment.

The Claimant is, however, permitted to accept compensation under a settlement negotiated on his behalf with a person or persons responsible, or with the Bureau. The vast majority of claims are in fact settled by negotiation with the Bureau.

17.   Legal rights unaffected

The scheme operated by the Motor Insurers' Bureau does not affect the legal rights of the parties concerned. The Claimant must prove his case at a court hearing and the Defendant (or Defender) ordered to pay the judgment. The Bureau then stands in the shoes of the successful Claimant, by the principle of subrogation, once it has paid out to the Claimant. It is entitled to recover from an otherwise impecunious Defendant who subsequently finds himself in funds, e.g., on winning the lottery, or receiving an inheritance.

Similarly, the insurers of the driver at fault retain their right to repudiate liability under their policy on the grounds that the conditions of the policy have been broken by the driver; or that the driver has failed to give due notice of the claim which has been made. It may well be that insurers could have rights to recover against their insured for such breaches of condition. The victim must, therefore, notify insurers, where they are known, and they will handle the claim in the usual way. In other words, the *insured* is not released from his contractual liability to his *insurer*, nor is he released from any liability in negligence to the third party victim.

18.   Handling claims

For the procedure for making a claim, see pp. 52 to 54.

The practice of the Bureau in cases where there is an insurance policy in existence, is for the *insurers* concerned to deal with the claim. This is so even where the claim does not fall within the terms of the policy — for example, where a car was being used for a purpose other than one for which it was insured, e.g., used for business when only insured for social use. This would not normally be the responsibility of the insurers, but, rather than deal with all claims itself, it is convenient for the Bureau to spread the workload by arranging for claims to be dealt with by the insurance companies and Lloyd's syndicates, who will in any event ultimately contribute to the Bureau's funds.

19.   Interim payments

Order 29, r. 11(2) of the Rules of the Supreme Court provides that no order for an interim payment is to be made if it appears to the court that the Defendant is not a person insured in respect of the claim, or a public authority, nor a person whose means and resources are such as to enable him to make such a payment. The Bureau clearly does not come within the first two categories, and the third is only capable of being relevant if the Bureau has (at its own instigation) been joined as a Defendant.

In *Powney* v *Coxage and Others, The Times*, 8 March 1988, Schiemann J held that the High Court had no jurisdiction to order the Bureau to make an interim payment under O. 29, r. 11 of the Rules of the Supreme Court. The basis for his decision was that the *potential* liability of the Bureau to make a payment was not a liability to pay damages to the plaintiff (who had sustained personal injuries when he had been struck by a vehicle driven by an uninsured driver). The interim payment sought was not within s. 32(5) of the Supreme Court Act 1981. The Bureau had been joined as a Defendant solely to enable it to defend the action on behalf of the other two Defendants. As the Bureau was not a Defendant who had admitted liability or against whom judgment had been obtained, and the plaintiff could not obtain judgment against the Bureau at the trial — there was no power to order an interim payment.

In *Sharp* v *Pereira, The Times*, 25 July 1998, the Master of the Rolls, giving judgment in the Court of Appeal, pointed out that, as a result of the *Powney* Case, O. 29, r. 11(2) was amended. He expressed the view that an interim payment order was a judgment within Clause 7 of the Uninsured Drivers Agreement 1988. If an interim payment order is not met by the judgment debtor within seven days, the Bureau would be liable to pay the sum ordered.

A Claimant's legal adviser or representative should therefore provide the Bureau with the information normally required by the court in applications for interim payments. The Bureau should thus be supplied with up to date medical reports, full details of the special damage claimed (for example, private hospital fees, loss of earnings, nursing costs, the cost of installing a chair-lift) and an explanation of the reason (special needs and hardship, for instance) for an interim payment. It should be noted that, as with applications to the court for interim payments, the remedy is a discretionary one, and the approach of the Bureau attempts to mirror that discretion in dealing with interim payment applications.

Although the above remarks applied to claims under the Uninsured Drivers Agreement 1988, it is understood that the Bureau's approach extends to interim payment applications arising out of untraced driver claims.

There has been a general tendency in recent years to move disputes away from the formalities of the Courts towards less formal means applied by the Tribunals and other judicial and quasi-judicial bodies. In a similar fashion, the Bureau is understood to consider each claim for an interim payment on its merits, applying principles similar to those applied by a Court. If the Bureau decides not to make an interim payment, application can be made to the court. (See Note 8 to the current Agreement.)

20.   The 'clawback' provisions

It should be noted that the Social Security Act 1990 provides for recovery (i.e., 'clawback') of benefits when compensation is paid by the Motor Insurers' Bureau on claims arising out of accidents caused by uninsured drivers.

Three

The 'Hit and Run' Motorist (The Untraced Drivers Agreement)

1. Introduction

During 1995, 1996 and 1997 (the latest available years) the number of prosecutions for failure to stop after a motor accident were 16,316, 15,736 and 15,829 respectively. To these may be added the prosecutions for failure to report such accidents within 24 hours, i.e., 13,922, 13,190 and 13,092. A number of police warnings were also given in appropriate circumstances when they were satisfied that there was sufficient evidence to satisfy a court, amounting to an additional 3,989, 3,862 and 3,575 for the same years. It is understood that two thirds of the prosecutions resulted in convictions for offences under s. 170 Road Traffic Act 1988. It must also be acknowledged that the many thousands of drivers who fail to stop after an accident escape prosecution simply because they are never traced. Many such accidents result in personal injury to an innocent victim who would have no redress were it not for the provisions for payment by the Motor Insurers' Bureau.

Even if the driver who caused an accident is traced and prosecuted, it may transpire that he was uninsured at the time, and again there might well be no compensation for the victim except under the Motor Insurers' Bureau's arrangements.

This chapter sets out how the Bureau provides compensation for those victims of drivers who are never traced.

2. The role of the Bureau

Under the original 1946 Agreement, the Bureau was under no *liability* to pay compensation to the victims in untraced motorist cases. It did, however, give 'sympathetic consideration' to claims made by victims where it was satisfied that there was a motor vehicle involved, and, apart from the fact that the vehicle, owner or driver could not be traced, a claim would lie in law. In many such cases, after giving 'sympathetic consideration' to the facts and the injuries, the Bureau made an *ex gratia* payment to the victim or, where the victim had died, to his dependants.

The 1969 Agreement extended the role of the Bureau in relation to untraced motorist cases, but did not otherwise affect its liabilities. 'Sympathetic consideration' was all that had been required under the 1946 Agreement. The Bureau thus had what amounted to a complete discretion whether or not to make a payment, and as to the amount of the payment. Later Agreements have imposed an *obligation* to deal with applications of this kind.

The 1969 Agreement applies to accidents which occurred on or after 1 May 1969 but before 1 December 1972. The 1972 Agreement applies to accidents which occurred on or after 1 December 1972. The 1996 Agreement applies to accidents on or after 1 July 1996 and is the current Agreement. It should be noted that the Bureau is under no liability to pay compensation for damage to property in respect of an accident caused by a 'hit and run' driver, that is, under the Untraced Drivers Agreement.

3. Making a claim

For the general procedure, see pp. 52 to 54. A claim arising out of an accident said to have been caused by an untraced driver must be made within three years of the accident.

On receiving the claim, the Bureau arranges for the circumstances of the accident to be investigated fully. When the investigation has taken place, the Bureau decides whether it will make an award, and, if so, the amount of the award. The decision of the Bureau is based broadly on common law principles of negligence as they apply to the accident.

In 1977, under the supplemental Agreement dated 7 December 1977, a procedure known as 'accelerated procedure' was introduced for applications for compensation by those injured in road accidents caused by *untraced* drivers and occurring on or after 3 January 1978. The procedure is less formal and speedier than the normal one. Claimants have the option of adopting either the accelerated or the normal procedure. The accelerated procedure does not apply to claims:

(a)   estimated to exceed £50,000 on full liability (this figure is revised from time to time) where the Claimant is legally represented; or

(b)   in which the Claimant is not adequately advised (that is, not legally represented) in claims estimated to exceed £5,000 on full liability; or

(c)   in which another identified driver is also involved; or

(d)   which present unusual features.

In cases dealt with under the accelerated procedure where the Claimant or his representatives agree to a negotiated settlement, the written consent of the Claimant is required. Payment will be made only after such consent is received. The effect of such consent is that the Claimant waives any right of appeal under the Agreement which is the procedure adopted when a discharge is obtained in the normal course of claims on the Bureau.

When the Bureau has reached a decision, that decision, together with reasons, and a statement setting out the circumstances of the accident and any facts relevant to the qualification of the award, is notified to the Claimant.

If the Claimant does not dispute the decision, or the amount of any award, within six weeks from notification of the decision, the award, if any, is paid by the Bureau.

4. Appeals

Except for claims settled under the accelerated procedure, a Claimant may dispute a decision of the Bureau not to make an award, or, if an award has been made, he may wish to dispute the amount. There is a right of appeal to an arbitrator selected from a panel of Queen's Counsel appointed by the Lord Chancellor. It is a prerequisite of an appeal that the parties will accept the decision of the arbitrator.

The statements and correspondence between the Claimant and the Bureau are forwarded to the arbitrator, who has power to ask the Bureau to investigate the claim further in order to clarify any matter raised. On the basis of the documents and having regard to the grounds of the appeal, the arbitrator then decides whether or not the Bureau should make an award, and, if so, the amount of the award.

The fee of the arbitrator is usually paid by the Bureau, unless the arbitrator decides, on the basis that there was no reasonable ground for the appeal and that it should be paid by the appellant.

It may be of note that since the inception of the scheme less than 2% of the decisions of the Bureau have been appealed against. A little over half of them have been successful.

It has already been noted that it is a prerequisite that the appellant agrees to accept the arbitrator's decision.

The fact that a notification of appeal disputing the decision of the Bureau has been forwarded to the Bureau does not preclude further consideration of the claim before an arbitrator is appointed. Such notification may give the Bureau an opportunity, before the file is sent to the arbitrator, to consider such matters as any fresh medical or other evidence which has come to light and which, had it been available earlier, might have led the Bureau to a different conclusion. Further consideration by the Bureau at this 'interim' stage may avoid the work and expense of a full appeal being dealt with by an arbitrator.

5. Other driver identified

The Bureau has the right to require that an identified driver, whom the Bureau considers to have been partly to blame for the accident, be sued, so that that driver's insurers may be called upon to pay the claim. The insurers will normally be liable at common law to pay the whole amount due to the Claimant, although their insured is only partly to blame, under the obligations of individual joint tortfeasors. This is in conformity with the Bureau's role as a 'body of last resort'.

If the known driver or other potential Defendant — a cyclist, for example — is uninsured and impecunious, the Bureau will not normally seek to involve him. It is for the Bureau to decide whether or not proceedings should be instituted, but it will insist upon such a course where it is reasonable to do so.

6. Injuries to passengers

Since 1 December 1972, when insurance cover for all passengers became compulsory, injuries to passengers are dealt with in the same way as other claims.

7. Costs

Pursuant to an understanding with The Law Society, the Bureau currently
pays the sum of £150 (+ VAT) towards solicitors' costs in addition to
reasonable disbursements (usually for police and medical reports, but
not, usually, Counsel's opinion) where a claim results in an award. When
one solicitor represents more than one applicant in claims arising from
the same accident, an additional fee of £75 will be paid for each
additional applicant. These sums are under review. The reason for the
rather nominal amount allowed is that the only work expected to be done
by a solicitor in an untraced motorist claim is normally restricted to
putting the Claimant in touch with the Bureau, which then carries out its
own investigation and advises the Claimant. As the Bureau can obtain
police reports free of charge, it will not usually reimburse Claimants or
their advisors for the fees they have paid for such reports.

8. No interest on awards

Until the 1999 Agreement there was no provision for interest on awards
relating to untraced driver claims. This topic was raised in answer to a
parliamentary question on 26 November 1986 when the Secretary of
State for Transport made the distinction between redress against a guilty
party and awards by the Bureau. He expressed his satisfaction at the
Bureau's practice which 'strikes a reasonable balance between Claimants
and the insured motorists who finance the Bureau through their
premiums'.

Notwithstanding this limitation, an arbitrator appointed by the Bureau
under the Agreement has the discretion to award interest in certain
circumstances (see *Evans* v *Motor Insurers' Bureau* at p. 50).

Clause 1 of the 1999 Agreement now provides for the Bureau's
obligations to pay interest.

9. 'Clawback' provisions

It should be noted that the Social Security Act 1990 provides for recovery
(i.e., 'clawback') of benefits when compensation is paid by the Motor
Insurers' Bureau on claims arising out of accidents caused by unidentified drivers.

10.   Checklist for untraced motorist claims

The following checklist should assist when investigating whether a claim is likely to succeed:

(a)   Consider evidence to show that the injury was caused by a motor vehicle (see pp. 48 to 49).

(b)   Consider evidence that the motor vehicle was on a road (see pp. 36 to 40).

(c)   Has there been a genuine inability to trace the driver, that is, have all reasonable efforts to trace the driver been made? (Some claims are rejected on the basis of insufficient evidence or of a long delay in carrying out an investigation.)

(d)   Were there any other parties involved? If other vehicles were involved, reasonable efforts must be made to trace the drivers.

(e)   Was there any contributory negligence on the part of the Claimant?

(f)   Does the evidence suggest a deliberate or concerted act by the driver to run down the victim? In such a case the possibility of a claim under the Criminal Injuries Compensation Scheme should be considered.

(g)   Is the claim made in time? Note that the Bureau has no discretion to extend the time for claiming beyond three years from the event.

(h)   Is the claim excluded? For example, was the vehicle involved a Crown vehicle? If so, a claim should be made against the government department under its own arrangements.

(i)   Should 'protective' proceedings be issued to preserve the victim's rights against the driver of any other known vehicle? Although this is primarily the responsibility of the Claimant or his advisers, not that of the Bureau, the Bureau should be kept fully informed (clause 11).

Four

The Green Card System

1. Introduction

The development of provision for the victims of road traffic accidents has not been confined to the United Kingdom. One of the problems to be met is that of providing compensation for a victim injured in one country by a motorist visiting from another country. The visitor could return to his own country and the success or failure of the victim's claim would depend on whether or not there were appropriate reciprocal arrangements between the two countries.

The matter was taken up in 1949 by the Inland Transport Committee of the Economic Commission for Europe at Geneva. The result of their deliberations was the emergence of the green card system, which came into force on 1 January 1953.

The Uniform Agreement between Bureaux has been in operation since 1 January 1991. It applies to accidents occurring on or after that date. For its terms and conditions to apply, a 'green card' international certificate of insurance must have been issued. The signatories to the Uniform Agreement are: Albania, Bosnia-Herzegovina, Bulgaria, Croatia, Estonia, Iran, Iraq (currently suspended), Israel, Latvia, the Former Yugoslav Republic of Macedonia (FYROM), Malta, Moldavia, Morocco, Poland, Slovenia, Tunisia, Turkey and Ukraine.

A 'green card' is required for a motorist travelling from the United Kingdom to the above countries.

For accidents occurring on or after 1 June 1991 there is in operation a Multilateral Guarantee Agreement signed between Member Bureaux.

It replaces earlier Supplementary Agreements. The signatories are: Austria, Belgium, Croatia, the Czech Republic, Denmark, Finland, France, Germany, Greece, Hungary, Iceland, Italy, Lichtenstein, Luxembourg, the Netherlands, Norway, Portugal, Slovakia, Slovenia, Spain, Sweden, Switzerland, and the United Kingdom.

The Multilateral Guarantee Agreement is based on the principle that the Bureau of the country in which the vehicle is normally based guarantees insurance against third party risks for travel in another signatory country. Thus it is proof that the minimum legal requirements for third party liability insurance in any country for which the green card is valid are covered by the insurer's *own* motor insurance policy.

It should be noted that the green card *itself* provides no insurance cover. Most insurance companies will issue one without charge. Some charge a nominal fee for the administrative expense of issuing the card. The UK Green Card Bureau at the Motor Insurers' Bureau, 152 Silbury Boulevard, Central Milton Keynes, MK9 1NB, tel: 01908 830001, may be contacted for general advice about the green card system.

2.   Operation of the green card scheme

Under the scheme, insurers in each country set up a Bureau, which has three purposes:

   (a)   to provide international motor insurance cards ('green cards') for issue to members of the Bureau or their policy-holders;
   (b)   as a *handling* Bureau to deal with claims brought against visiting motorists who carry green cards;
   (c)   as a *paying* Bureau to meet the claims of handling Bureaux.

Where there is a green card, the relevant vehicle is deemed to be insured, even if it is not. The green card is evidence of a policy of insurance issued in accordance with the compulsory third party insurance law of the country visited and is accepted as sufficient compliance with that law. The signature on the green card by the policy-holder authorises the handling Bureau to settle third party claims in accordance with the law of the country visited.

The various national Bureaux enter into agreements with each other, under which arrangements are made for the 'handling Bureau' to be reimbursed by the appropriate 'paying Bureau'.

The Motor Insurers' Bureau is both the handling Bureau and the paying Bureau for the United Kingdom. The secretariat for the Council of Bureaux, a body established by motor insurers in Europe to administer the green card system, is an independent body located in London. The Secretary-General is Mr M Nicholson.

3. Foreign motorists in the UK

The responsibility of the Motor Insurers' Bureau to satisfy any judgment in respect of a liability compulsorily insurable but not in fact insured has been examined in Chapter 2. The nationality of the Defendant in question is of no relevance, and, therefore, everything that has been said in Chapter 2 applies regardless of the nationality or domicile of the motorist at fault. However, where the foreign negligent motorist is the holder of a valid green card, the Motor Insurers' Bureau, following settlement of claim by it, is able to recover its outlay from the foreign insurer which issued the green card, or, failing that, from the Bureau which provided the green card.

Persons who sustain injury as a result of the negligence of foreign motorists should, as soon as practicable after the accident, give notice to the Motor Insurers' Bureau of the nature of the claim and the name of the person against whom that claim is made. It is also of considerable assistance to the Bureau if the registration number of the offending vehicle can be given, together with the number and period of validity of the green card, if there is one.

Claims against foreign motorists in respect of accidents occurring on or after 31 December 1988 may include claims for damage to property as well as for personal injury (see pp. 15 *et seq*).

4. British motorists abroad

British motorists involved in accidents in other countries which have adopted the green card system are required to notify the accident to their insurer's appointed representative in that country, or to the local (National) Bureau. Where there is no local representative, a claim which falls within the ambit of the local (national) compulsory third party insurance law will be disposed of by the Bureau in that country. It will then seek reimbursement of its outlay from the insurer in the United Kingdom which issued the green card, or from the Motor Insurers' Bureau itself. It should be noted that the third Motor Directive requires that, since 1993, the 'home' third party cover must apply if wider than the cover required under local legislation.

The Motor Insurers' Bureau, together with the majority of other Bureaux of the Green Card System, are signatories to the 'Protection of Visitors Agreement'. Under that Agreement a service is offered by the Bureau to UK citizens injured or suffering damage to property in a road accident. The service offered is restricted to supplying information and documentation on payment of a small administration charge and any disbursements. The service will also provide information about English speaking lawyers in the country involved. The Bureau will not handle the claims.

5. Green cards in the United Kingdom

The effect of having a green card in the United Kingdom is dealt with by the Motor Vehicles (Compulsory Insurance) No. 2 Regulations 1973; the Motor Vehicles (Third Party Rules Amendment) Regulations 1973; the Motor Vehicles (Third Party Rights Amendment) Regulations 1974 and the Motor Vehicles Compulsory Insurance No. 2 (Amendment) Regulations 1974.

6. Inspection of green cards at frontiers

One of the reasons for setting up the green card system in the first place was so that the motorist should not be impeded in his journey by the need to comply with the differing insurance requirements of each country visited. The convenience of the motorist was taken into account by a decision not to inspect green cards at the internal frontiers of the countries of the European Community. The only countries in the European Community that still require such inspections are France (on occasions) and Spain in respect of the border with Gibraltar.

7. Differences in insurance provisions

Notwithstanding the increasing rationalisation of insurance provision between the states of the European Union, there are still substantial differences between the levels of insurance cover required by law, the manner in which claims are handled and the amount of money a victim may be entitled to receive. Travellers abroad should make sure that their own insurance cover is not only sufficient to satisfy the legal requirements of the country visited but to provide adequate compensation if they become victims of an accident.

This function will be superceded in the near future by the Fourth Motor Insurance Directive which will require motor insurers in the European Economic Area to have a representative in every other country in the Area authorised to handle claims made by citizens of that country irrespective of where the accident occurred. The Directive also provides for a compensation body to take over the handling of a claim where there is no representation or one proves to be incompetant. In the United Kingdom the compensation body will be the Motor Insurers' Bureau.

Five

Rights Against Insurers

1. The statutory provisions

Sections 151 and 152 of the Road Traffic Act 1988 provide that an insurer may have to meet a liability under a policy even though the insurer is entitled to avoid or cancel the policy because, for example, the policy was obtained on the basis of non-disclosure of a material fact or by misrepresentation. Where the policy-holder in such a case has caused an accident, the victim of that accident can sue the driver and has a right to recover payment of damages and costs from that driver's insurer. The victim must give notice of the bringing of proceedings to the insurer, either before, or within seven days after, the institution of the proceedings against the driver.

The insurer can avoid any obligation to pay only by obtaining from a court a declaration that he is entitled to avoid the policy on the ground, for example, that it was obtained by non-disclosure of a material fact or misrepresentation. Also, before or within seven days of starting the action seeking the declaration, the victim must be notified that this is done specifying the grounds for seeking to avoid the policy. The victim is then entitled to become a party to that action.

These provisions have in part been rendered superfluous by the Motor Insurers' Bureau Agreement, but there are some circumstances in which they remain relevant.

2. Proceedings by Claimant against insurers

A victim is pursuing a claim for personal injuries arising out of a motor accident. The insurers dealing with the claim on behalf of the negligent driver are dilatory. Notice required under the 1988 Act is given to the insurers by the solicitors acting for the Claimant. The insurers give no assistance to the solicitors with regard to acceptance of service of proceedings on the insurers' negligent driver. In those circumstances the solicitors quite properly serve the driver personally. He may fail to pass the writ to the insurers, or may take no steps to defend the proceedings. The solicitors would then be in a position to obtain judgment in default of appearance and damages would be assessed by the court.

In such a case it is possible for the Claimant's adviser to seek payment of the judgment debt from the Motor Insurers' Bureau if the required notice has been given to the Bureau under clause 9 (see p. 65). The alternative course is to pursue the claim against the insurers under s. 152, Road Traffic Act 1988.

If no such notice has been given to the Bureau, or if the Bureau decides not to waive the requirement that notice be given to it, the Claimant may pursue his remedy under s. 152 of the Road Traffic Act 1988 against the insurers themselves.

As a general rule, however, insurance companies are not dilatory in dealing with claims, and drivers normally are sufficiently aware of their duty to pass on all relevant communications to their insurers.

Even so, errors and delay are not unknown. Drivers may fail to pass on relevant communications to their insurers merely because they feel the accident was not their responsibility, or they may have mislaid the communication. They may also feel (however erroneously) that, having notified their insurers of the actual claim, they need not pass on any further communications with regard to it.

In events, or a combination of events, such as these, the procedure outlined for claims against insurers may be followed. It is worthy of note that in 1998 the Law Commission issued a consultation paper on the Third Parties (Rights Against Insurers) Act 1930. One of its suggestions was that, in some circumstances, the liability of an insured party and that of the insurer would be dealt with in one set of proceedings. Other suggestions relate to disclosure of policy information and the ability of insurers to rely on breaches of conditions in the policy.

Six

Resolution of Differences between the Bureau and its Members in Joint Tortfeasor Claims

Those with experience in the appropriate field of law will be aware of the 'Bridlington Agreement' for resolving differences between unions (and between members and unions). By analogy the Bureau has its own procedure, introduced since 1981, to provide an expeditious and cost-saving facility for dealing with the determination of liability as between the Central Fund of the Bureau and a member or members in appropriate cases. Under clause 6(1)(6) of the Untraced Drivers Agreement 1996 a Claimant may be required by the Bureau to take all reasonable steps to obtain judgment against another known driver (or drivers) as joint tortfeasor with the untraced driver. In such cases the Bureau affords an indemnity for the costs thus incurred.

Many with a valid claim, in particular innocent victims, may, as a result of the procedure, be compensated more speedily and without the stressful need for litigation. Courts have made adverse comments in judgments, as well as during hearings, about what is seen by judges and public alike as an unseemly wrangle within the insurance industry. This often results in an injured party (or the family of a Claimant who has died as a result of the injuries) being denied compensation for an unconscionable length of time (see *Liff* v *Peasley* [1980] 1 All ER 623).

The costs of protracted disputes between the Bureau and its members is minimised by the substitution of an informal arbitration procedure dealt with by documents only.

It is for the relevant Bureau Committee and *not* for the individual investigating member, to decide whether this procedure should be applied. However, an individual investigating member, during the course of the investigation, may consider it appropriate for that member or another member (or members) upon whom liability *may* fall, to dispose of the claim as a prudent practical measure. It is then for the Bureau to decide whether the procedure should be invoked. An early reference on the facts by the investigating member is the most sensible course. Liability can then be conclusively determined.

It is standard procedure for the facts to be set out by the investigating member in an interim report which is considered by a Bureau Committee. If those facts indicate the making of some award, the Committee will invite the member who applied to take over the claim for settlement. This will also be appropriate where clause 6(1)(b) (see p. 80) would otherwise have applied. If such an invitation is not accepted, the procedure outlined above will be applied.

The investigating member can be asked to dispose of the claim by way of the 'accelerated procedure' (see pp. 17–18) or to report as soon as possible to the Bureau for an award to be made. The latter course is the more appropriate one in most cases. If an arbitrator later finds against the member, the Bureau will then be reimbursed by such member.

The arbitrator is normally selected from a panel of QC's appointed under the Agreement, thus ensuring familiarity with, and experience of, the practice of the Bureau. The arbitrator is supplied with the investigating member's report, to which are added any further material and comments from the Bureau and the member. The arbitrator is normally asked to reach a decision on one simple issue, i.e., whether any legal liability rests on the person for whom the member is responsible. The decision of the arbitrator is binding and costs usually follow the event, as would normally be the practice in the courts.

In some cases, the only issue the arbitrator has to decide is whether the individual concerned has been adequately identified as the driver responsible for the accident (see pp. 34–36 for reference to case law on 'identity problems'). If the case is one of exceptional difficulty as between the member and its policy holder, the investigating member may find it appropriate to deal with the case on the basis of an 'untraced driver' claim, with the issue of liability being determined later under the procedure.

Solicitors representing Claimants may find themselves in a difficult and complex dilemma when, after proceedings are issued and served, a defence is served seeking to blame an untraced motorist as the sole person responsible for the accident. In such circumstances, solicitors may notify the Bureau of a claim under the Untraced Drivers Agreement by way of a 'belt and braces' tactic. The danger in not doing so may be that, at the end of the day (or days) in court, the plaintiff's claim, against the known driver fails and any claim on Bureau funds under the Untraced Drivers Agreement could well be out of time.

There is no provision in the Bureau Agreements for 'provisional' claims being made and held in abeyance pending resolution of the litigation analogous to a writ or summons being issued to preserve a Claimant's rights — known in legal circles as a 'protective' writ or summons, now known as a 'claim form' in England and Wales. In order to bring matters to a head, solicitors are asked by the Bureau whether or not their client is making a claim under the Untraced Drivers Agreement. If they indicate that such is the case, the claim is then referred to an investigating member.

In a small number of cases where the situation is complicated, the Bureau has to make a pragmatic decision on the best course to follow. A claim may then be investigated on the basis that any legal proceedings against a known Defendant are stayed. An award can then only be made if the Bureau is satisfied that the untraced motorist was fully to blame (subject, of course, to any reduction to take account of the Claimant's own contributory negligence, if appropriate). Acceptance of an award made by the Bureau carries with it the ending of the stayed proceedings against the (known) Defendant. Nevertheless it would be technically possible (though perhaps morally reprehensible) for a Claimant, after collecting an award from the Bureau, to continue the proceedings against the known Defendant. In any event, under the terms set out on the Bureau's form of receipt and discharge, any damages recovered in the litigation would have to be refunded by the Claimant to the Bureau.

Seven

Cases Involving or Affecting the Motor Insurers' Bureau

This chapter deals with the attitude taken by the courts to the activities of the Bureau in the interpretation of the Motor Insurers' Bureau Agreements and also the approach taken by the Bureau with regard to claims made under the Agreements. A few cases affecting the Bureau's activities are included, although the Bureau was not a party to the proceedings giving rise to the judgments.

1. Strictness of interpretation

The first group of cases deals with claims made against the Bureau under clause 1 of the 1946 Agreement and illustrates the types of defence which had been raised by the Bureau, quite properly, in an endeavour to show such claims to be outside the scope of the Agreement.

In *Buchanan* v *Motor Insurers' Bureau* [1955] 1 All ER 607, [1955] 1 WLR 488, 99 SJ 319, the plaintiff had successfully sued a lorry driver for negligence. The accident had occurred on premises belonging to the Port of London Authority and the point taken was whether these constituted a 'road' for the purposes of the Road Traffic Acts. If it did, the Bureau would be liable. McNair J gave judgment for the Defendant on the basis that the road in question was not a road within the meaning of the Road Traffic Acts, as it was not in a place to which the general public had access by right or by tolerance of the Port of London Authority.

The view may be taken that the Bureau had adopted an attitude more akin to the strict letter of the law rather than in accordance with the intention of the Motor Insurers' Bureau Agreement. This was reflected in the judgment of McNair J when he said: 'Apparently it is thought right on behalf of the Defendants to take this point and all I can say is that, in law, it is a good point.' It may, however, be maintained that the Bureau had simply followed the established practice of insurers of bringing or defending borderline cases in order to establish on which side of the line the case falls.

2. Liability not accepted where passenger not compulsorily insurable

Other examples of cases defended by the Bureau which establish the extent of its liability, include *Coward* v *Motor Insurers' Bureau* [1963] 1 QB 259, [1962] 1 All ER 531, [1962] 2 WLR 663; *Connell* v *Motor Insurers' Bureau* [1969] 2 QB 494, [1969] 3 All ER 572, [1969] 3 WLR 231; *Albert* v *Motor Insurers' Bureau* [1972] AC 301, [1971] 2 All ER 1345, [1971] 3 WLR 291; and *Motor Insurers' Bureau* v *Meanan* [1971] 2 All ER 1372. All these cases revolved round whether or not in the circumstances a passenger was being carried for hire and reward so as to render liability for the passenger compulsorily insurable. The point is now of academic interest only, as since 1 December 1972, it is obligatory to insure liability for all passengers.

3. Criminal use of vehicle

What follows must now be read in the light of clause 6(e)(iii) of the 1999 Uninsured Drivers Agreement.

In *Hardy* v *Motor Insurers' Bureau* [1964] 2 QB 745, [1964] 2 All ER 742, [1964] 3 WLR 433, a security officer, noticing a stolen road fund licence on a van belonging to a fitter, waited for the van at a point where the private road through his employers' property joined the main road. He tried to stop the driver by putting his head in at the window and asking the driver to pull up at the side of the road. The driver drove off at speed, dragging the plaintiff on his knees to the main road. The security officer fell off while the car was on the main road. The driver was charged with, and found guilty of, driving without a licence or insurance and causing grievous bodily harm. In subsequent civil proceedings against the driver, judgment was entered by consent for £300 damages.

The judgment being unsatisfied, the plaintiff brought proceedings against the Motor Insurers' Bureau, which defended the claim on the basis that the claim arose out of a wilful and deliberate criminal act and that, as such, the claim would not be covered by a policy of insurance, even had there been such a policy in existence.

The Court of Appeal held that insurance cover, being compulsory for liability arising out of the use of the vehicle by the insured on a road, would include 'murderous' or 'playful' use. Therefore, even though the driver was guilty of a felony under s. 18 of the Offences against the Person Act 1861, and, as between the insurer and the driver, liability might have been denied (i.e., the driver could not recover from his insurers), this would not have affected the plaintiff's claim against the driver himself and, under s. 207 of the Road Traffic Act 1960 (now s. 151 of the Road Traffic Act 1988; see pp. 27 to 28), the plaintiff would have had a right against the insurers, notwithstanding the fact that the claim arose out of the 'wilful and culpable criminal act' of the insured.

Diplock LJ, in the course of his judgment, drew attention to the point that there was no cause of action disclosed in the statement of claim against the Motor Insurers' Bureau. It was pointed out that it was not the practice of the Bureau, in dealing with this type of claim, to take the point that there is no legal liability to the *Claimant*, the liability of the Bureau being only to the Secretary of State for Transport (now the Secretary of State for Environment, Transport and the Regions). No claim has been recorded against the Minister or his successor for a declaration of specific performance of the Agreement.

In *Gardner* v *Moore* [1984] AC 548 the House of Lords, in declining an invitation to overrule *Hardy* v *Motor Insurers' Bureau*, held the Bureau liable to pay damages to a pedestrian deliberately run down by a driver who later pleaded guilty to a charge under s. 18 of the Offences Against the Person Act 1861. However, it was recognised that a victim had an option to approach *either* the Bureau *or* make a claim under the Criminal Injuries Compensation Scheme. It was also noted that clause 1(1)(e) of the then current Untraced Drivers Agreement excluded from the Bureau's jurisdiction deliberate injury claims in the 'hit and run' context.

4.   Identity problems

Identifying the driver involved in an incident giving rise to a claim is of vital importance in most civil and criminal cases. In *Scarsbrook and*

Others v *Mason* [1961] 3 All ER 767 the plaintiffs were injured while standing on a footpath when a car was driven so fast round a bend that the driver lost control of it and knocked them down. A jacket belonging to the Defendant had been found after the incident, caught in the offside rear door of the car. He stated that he had accepted the invitation of the other occupant of the car to go for a ride and had paid four shillings as a contribution towards petrol. His evidence was that he was not the driver of the car and he did not know who the driver was. The judge held that the occupants were 'jointly and severally liable for the manner in which the motor car was driven, *viz*, that it was driven negligently and the plaintiffs are entitled to succeed against this member of the party on the ground that the driver was acting as agent for each and all the members of that party'. This principle applies *a fortiori* when the persons using the vehicle are doing so in pursuance of some joint unlawful purpose.

Another case involved an inference as to the identity of the driver. A driver of a blue Range Rover (which had not been identified by its number plate) admitted that he had been driving in the vicinity at the time of the incident. A blue Range Rover had 'cut up' a Volkswagen on Finchley Road, London, forcing it to swerve and hit another motor car. The driver of the Range Rover continued his journey without stopping. A conviction for driving without due care was upheld on appeal. The magistrates at first instance were entitled, on the facts, to draw the inference that the accused driver was the one involved.

As far back as *Monk* v *Warbey and Others* [1934] All ER 373, the Court of Appeal held that a person injured as a result of a breach of the relevant statutory provisions has a *prima facie* right to recover damages from the person breaking those provisions. In that case the owner of the vehicle had lent it to a person who was not insured for third party risks. In permitting such user, the owner was in breach of what is now re-enacted as s. 143(1) of the Road Traffic Act 1988. The plaintiff was awarded damages against the owner on the basis that he had permitted the uninsured use of the vehicle.

In *Rogers* v *Night Riders (a firm)* [1983] RTR 324, a minicab firm was held by the Court of Appeal to be under a duty to ensure not only that it provided cars properly maintained and reasonably fit for the purpose of conveying customers safely to their destinations, but also to provide drivers fit for that purpose. During the plaintiff's journey, a side door flew open, hit a stationary vehicle and rebounded hitting the plaintiff. The driver could not be traced and an action against him was discontinued. The minicab firm was held liable on the basis that the vehicle was defective, and the firm was in breach of the duty to take reasonable steps to ensure that the vehicle was properly maintained and reasonably fit for the stated purpose. That could not be delegated to the driver, whether he was an employee or an independent contractor.

Ownership of a vehicle is *prima facie* evidence that it was being driven at the material time by the owner or his servant or agent. Thus, in the unreported case of *Pask and Another* v *Keefe and Another* (Webster J in the Queen's Bench Division on 25 April 1985), although it was not conclusively proved that the Defendant was the driver of the taxi, judgment was nevertheless entered against the owners of the taxi.

5.   Injury by vehicle on a 'road'

The question of whether or not a motor vehicle has been in use on a road does not arise in the usual run of accident cases. This is because the user or owner of a vehicle is normally insured for legal liability to third parties for claims arising out of accidents in which the vehicle is involved, irrespective of whether the vehicle was on a public highway or on private property.

However, this is a matter of concern to the Bureau because its liability under the Agreements is restricted to the use of a vehicle on a road within the definition contained in s. 192 of the Road Traffic Act 1988. The Act defines a 'road' as 'any highway and any other road to which the public has access, and includes bridges over which a road passes'. A similar definition is to be found in the Road Traffic Act (Northern Ireland) Order 1981.

Most reported cases (and there are many) relate to prosecutions in the magistrates' courts for such offences as use of a vehicle without a current MOT certificate; parking without lights; or driving an unroadworthy vehicle — all involving a vehicle being used on a 'road'.

In order to establish that a vehicle is on a 'road' within the statutory definition, it must be on a road (in the ordinary non-technical sense of the word) to which the public has access. In *Oxford* v *Austin* [1981] RTR 416 (Divisional Court), Kilner Brown J approached the problem in two parts. He said 'The first question which has to be asked is whether there is in fact in the ordinary understanding of the word a road, that is to say, whether or not there is a definable way between the two points over which vehicles could pass. The second question is whether or not the public, or a section of the public, has access to that which has the appearance of a definable way. If both questions can be answered affirmatively, there is a road for the purposes of the various Road Traffic Acts and Regulations.'

The approach to the definition of a 'road to which the public has access' had been given consideration in the much earlier case of *Harrison v Hill* [1932] SC(J) 13 where Lord Clyde applied a test of whether or not 'the public actually and legally enjoys access to it'. He included access which was 'permitted or allowed, expressly or implicitly, by the person ... to whom the road belongs', and such cases involving 'tolerance of a proprietor' would come within the definition. Such an approach has been expressly approved in *Buchanan* v *Motor Insurers' Bureau* [1955] 1 All ER 607, *Adams* v *Commissioner of Police* [1980] RTR 289, and in the Divisional Court judgments in *Bugge* v *Taylor* [1941] 1 KB 198 and *Griffin* v *Squires* [1958] 3 All ER 468 (see below).

Difficulties of interpretation of the term 'road' arise in relation to such places as courtyards, forecourts, short cuts, lanes giving access to farms, and roads on industrial estates. The question for the court is one of fact in the circumstances of each particular case. In *Bugge* v *Taylor*, the public used a forecourt as a short cut. This was held to be a road. However, in *Thomas* v *Dando* [1951] 1 All ER 1010, a particular forecourt was held not to be a road. The court held in *Griffin* v *Squires* [1958] 3 All ER 468 that a car park providing access for allotment holders and members of a private bowling club to a private path leading to the club was not a road.

It should be noted that, unusually, the courts have not adopted the Oxford Dictionary definition, which is 'a line of communication between places for the use of foot passengers, riders and vehicles'. In *Griffin* v *Squires*, Streatfield J said, 'I have to give proper effect to the words of the Act of Parliament. Although a car park is, in my opinion, a line of communication, I do not think that anybody in the ordinary acceptance of the word "road" would think of a car park as a road. If we were to hold that this was a road, a piece of waste land by the side of the road to which the public could resort for picnics would also have to be a road, and nobody would call that a road.'

Further guidance is provided by the judgment in *Purves* v *Muir* [1948] JC 122 where examples of roads were given, including a farm road to which the public has access, a drive leading from a public road up to a private house, and a forecourt at the entrance to an hotel where there was open access from both sides. An essential criterion is whether or not the public has access to them.

It is understood that an arbitrator, in an MIB claim in Scotland, following the *Purves* v *Muir* judgment, held that an underpass intended for use by pedestrians only, with a space of only four feet between bollards, was not a 'road' within the definition we have been examining.

Another arbitrator (in England) decided that a paved area owned by the Greater London Council, which had not expressly or implicitly permitted the driving of vehicles over it, was not a road. On the other hand, the same arbitrator accepted that a tow path was within the definition of a 'road' and therefore within the scope of the Untraced Drivers Agreement.

In another MIB arbitration, the status of an open beach was considered. It was decided that it was not a road as compulsory third party insurance was not required with regard to that particular beach. The position would probably be different where a defined and tangible route of communication over the surface of a beach is involved.

A road on Forestry Commission land with gates intended to exclude vehicles driven by the public was held by another arbitrator not to be a 'road' within the definition.

In *Sadiku* v *Director of Public Prosecutions, The Times*, 3 December 1999 the Queen's Bench Divisional Court was called upon to decide whether Trafalgar Square is a road. Quite unsurprisingly the Court held that it is, reiterating that a decision whether or not a particular place is a road was one for the magistrates at first instance. Incidentally, new regulations are expected in the not too distant future to clarify the definition of a road under the Road Traffic legislation.

It should be noted that views expressed by the police as to whether or not a particular road comes within the statutory definition may be relevant, or even persuasive, but they are not binding on the Bureau.

In *Randall* v *Motor Insurers' Bureau* [1969] 1 All ER 21, [1968] 1 WLR 1900, 112 SJ 883, a school sergeant had been instructed by the headmaster of the school to see that a site, which was being cleared for building at the rear of the school, was not used for further unauthorised tipping of rubbish.

A lorry driver was about twelve yards onto the site when Mr Randall told him that he would be reported to the police. The lorry driver became abusive and Mr Randall walked to the side entrance. The lorry driver moved forward, straight at Mr Randall, with the engine roaring. Mr Randall jumped to his left, but was caught on his right leg by the lorry's wing and trapped between the moving lorry and the escarpment of a raised bank. This initially caused no substantial injury but, as the lorry passed him, he was pulled forward and fell to the ground. The offside rear wheel of the lorry went over his left leg, while the front wheels were well out into the road. The lorry driver then drove off.

The lorry driver was prosecuted to conviction and Mr Randall obtained judgment in a civil action against him for damages assessed at £1,073 and costs, which were taxed at £243. The Bureau had notice of the proceedings. The lorry driver's insurers repudiated liability and the Bureau, in accordance with its usual practice in such cases, to save unnecessary costs of third party litigation, agreed that the action could be brought against it without the insurers being joined.

After consideration the definition of a 'road', as set out in the Road Traffic Act 1960 (which applied at the time and which has now been replaced by s. 192 of the Road Traffic Act 1988), and whether the lorry had been used on a road in the particular case, Megaw J held that the injuries arose out of the use of a vehicle on the road and that the damages awarded under the judgment against the lorry driver were therefore recoverable under the Motor Insurers' Bureau Agreement.

6.   Car park not normally a road

In *Clarke* v *Kato* and *Cutter* v *Eagle Star Insurance Company Limited* (1998) *The Times*, 23 October, the House of Lords, allowing appeals from the Court of Appeal '... would hesitate to formulate a comprehensive definition where by a place might be identified as a road, but some guidance might be found by considering its physical character and the function it existed to serve'. Any judgment on the definition of a road boiled down to a discussion on the facts of each case.

The House of Lords considered that a car park does not qualify, using ordinary language, as a 'road' either in 'character and more especially in function; the two were distinct'. It defined the functions of a road as enabling *movement* to a destination and only incidentally would a vehicle be *stationary* while on it. It could be used for parking. A car park was to enable vehicles to *stand* and *wait*. Driving across it was only incidental to its principal function.

Some other examples were highlighted in the judgment which will no doubt be cited in argument in future cases. They include a hard shoulder which 'might be seen to form part of a road' and a lay-by giving rise to 'a more delicate question'. The House of Lords expressly excluded a car park from being regarded as a road in all but exceptional circumstances.

Reference had been made in argument at the hearing to three European Directives (72/166 EEC, 84/5 EEC and 90/232 EEC) but the Court held that there was nothing relevant to be included in the definition of a road.

The next two cases deal with miscellaneous points arising out of the activities of the Bureau.

7. Owner's liability where Bureau pays damages against driver

In *Corfield* v *Groves* [1950] 1 All ER 488, 94 SJ 225, a man was fatally injured as a result of the negligence of an uninsured driver, who had been driving a vehicle which did not belong to him. The dead man's widow and only dependant sued the driver for negligence and also claimed against the owner of the vehicle for breach of statutory duty, as the driver was without means to satisfy any judgment obtained against him.

A representative of the Motor Insurers' Bureau was called as a witness and stated that, under the Motor Insurers' Bureau Agreement, it would satisfy any judgment against the driver. The owner of the vehicle, who was not the master or principal of the driver, contended that, as the Bureau would pay damages, the widow would suffer no loss arising out of the driver's lack of means or the alleged breach of statutory duty. Hilbery J held that, as the widow's right accrued immediately on the death of her husband, she had an enforceable claim against the owner of the vehicle for any damages suffered arising out of the breach of statutory duty existing at the time of the negligence. He therefore gave judgment against both Defendants. (On the basis that the judgment was to be satisfied by the Bureau, the plaintiff could not, of course, recover twice!)

8. Bureau's support of assisted Defendant relevant on costs

In *Godfrey and Another* v *Smith and Another* [1955] 2 All ER 520, [1955] 1 WLR 692, 99 SJ 419, proceedings were brought against an uninsured motor cyclist by another motor cyclist and his pillion passenger, arising out of a collision between the two vehicles. The uninsured motor cyclist became legally aided after judgment, but the plaintiffs were at no time legally aided. Application was then made for costs to be assessed by the judge. The case came before Donovan J, who felt that, if the Bureau had not been 'behind the Defendant' (that is, if the Bureau had not taken over the defence), he would have made an order for £50 by instalments. It would be unfair to the plaintiff for him to be out of pocket because the Defendant was legally aided and not in a position to pay the costs in one lump sum. The judge therefore took the Motor Insurers' Bureau Agreement into account and ordered payment of the taxed costs in the usual way.

9.   Application by Bureau to be added as Defendant and substituted service

It should be noted that the liability of the Bureau under the various Agreements is to the Secretary of State and not to the victim. This point is not taken by the Bureau but it has sometimes been raised by other parties to litigation involving the Bureau, as is illustrated by the following cases.

In *Fire Auto and Marine Insurance Co. Ltd* v *Greene* [1964] 2 QB 687, [1964] 2 All ER 761, [1964] 3 WLR 319, the insurers of a driver began an action under s. 207(3) of the Road Traffic Act 1960 (now re-enacted as s. 152 of the Road Traffic Act 1988), claiming a declaration that they were entitled to avoid their policy with him on the ground that he had failed to disclose a material fact. A claim had been brought arising out of an accident involving the driver. The insurers were not members of the Motor Insurers' Bureau. The Bureau applied, under O. 15, r. 6 of the Rules of the Supreme Court, to be added as Defendants in the action. They argued that, under the 1946 Motor Insurers' Bureau Agreement, clause 1, the Bureau would be required to meet any judgment obtained by the victim against the insurers, if the insurers were successful in obtaining a declaration. Under that rule, the court has a discretion to 'order any person who ought to have been joined as a party or whose presence before the court is necessary to ensure that all matters in dispute (in the action) may be effectually and completely determined and adjudicated upon,' to be added as a party.

Stephenson J held that the Bureau was not entitled to be joined as a party, on the basis that it had not shown that some legal right enforceable by it against one of the parties to the action, or some legal duty enforceable against one of the parties to the action, or some legal duty enforceable against the Bureau by one of the parties to the action, would be affected by the result of the action. The case seemed to turn on the fact that the insurers were not members of the Motor Insurers' Bureau under the 'domestic' agreement. Even if the Bureau were legally liable to satisfy the judgment against the insured, the Bureau would not be liable to anyone other than, perhaps, the Secretary of State for Transport and certainly not to the Claimant himself. The Bureau had never taken the point against the Claimant, but that did not prevent the insurers in the action from taking the point against the Bureau. The legal position of the Bureau was examined carefully and its liability was found to be contractual and to confer legal rights on the Minister only.

This decision has, however, been criticised in *Gurtner* v *Circuit* [1968] 2 QB 587, [1968] 1 All ER 328, [1968] 2 WLR 668. In that case, a pedestrian sustained injuries, including a fractured skull and loss of memory, as a result of being knocked down by a motorist. The motorist gave certain details to the police including his address and the number of the policy or cover note which he described as being 'with Lloyd's'. Those acting for the plaintiff in connection with the claim were rather slow in proceeding with it. A writ was issued and renewed during the time they were inquiring into and investigating the accident generally and, in particular, the whereabouts of the Defendant. When eventually inquiries were made by the process servers endeavouring to serve the writ at the address given by the Defendant to the police at the time of the accident, they were informed that the Defendant had emigrated to Canada some two years before, leaving no trace of a forwarding address.

The Motor Insurers' Bureau was notified of the claim and it delegated the investigation to an insurance company, in accordance with its usual practice. The insurance company was also unsuccessful in tracing the Defendant or his insurers. The plaintiff had dispensed with his solicitors and was, by that time, acting in person. Dissatisfied with the lack of progress, he applied to the court for an order for substituted service, and it was ordered that the Defendant could be served by sending a copy of the writ to the registered office of the insurance company who were investigating the claim on behalf of the Motor Insurers' Bureau.

The writ having been served in accordance with the order, the Bureau applied to be added as Defendants to enable the Bureau to stand in the shoes, as it were, of the Defendant, and to protect its financial interests. It wished to have the renewal of the writ and the order for substituted service set aside. It also wished to take advantage of the fact that no notice had been given by the plaintiff to it within 21 days of the institution of proceedings as was required by clause 5 of the 1946 Motor Insurers' Bureau Agreement. An order was made allowing the Bureau to be added as Defendant on an undertaking to satisfy any damages awarded to the plaintiff arising out of the Defendant's negligence, but without prejudice to the Bureau's right to defend on other grounds. At the same time the orders renewing the writ, the order for substituted service, and the service in accordance with the former order, were set aside. The plaintiff's appeal against these later orders was allowed. The judge took the view that he was bound by the ruling in the case of *Fire Auto and Marine Insurance Co. Ltd* v *Greene* (see p. 41).

The case then went to the Court of Appeal, where Lord Denning MR felt that the *Fire Auto and Marine* case was wrong and should be overruled. He considered that O. 15, r. 6 applied to the type of situation in which the Bureau found itself. He therefore reinstated the original orders insofar as they allowed the Bureau to be added as a Defendant in the proceedings. He made it a condition that the counter-claim made by the Bureau, i.e., that the time element in clause 5 had not been complied with, should not be allowed to be pleaded in the proceedings.

Diplock LJ in the course of his judgment agreeing with the Master of the Rolls, made a very practical and sensible suggestion that in special circumstances, as occurred in this case, there being *prima facie* evidence that the Defendant was insured, there could really be no harm in ordering substituted service, *not* on the insurance company nominated by the Bureau to investigate the case, but on the Bureau itself. He felt that such an order should only be made if all other efforts failed.

In *Clarke and Another* v *Vedel and Another* (1979) RTR 26, CA, a differently constituted Court of Appeal dismissed an appeal from Jupp J, pointing out that the general principle applicable in making orders for substituted service was that the effect of the order was that it was likely that the writ would reach the Defendant. In road traffic cases, there might be exceptions where a Defendant could be ordered to be served at the address of his insurers or the Bureau if he could not be traced and was unlikely to be reached by *any* form of substituted service. The case where a man had given completely false information as to his name and address, and possibly his age, and had probably stolen the vehicle he had driven causing the personal injuries, did not fall within the exception. The effect of the decision was that the Claimants could continue to claim against the Bureau under the *Untraced* Drivers Agreement but *not* under the Uninsured Driver Agreement. The difference in treatment of the claim would be that, under that *Uninsured* Drivers Agreement, the Bureau would be liable to pay the amount of the judgment after a hearing, whereas under the Untraced Drivers Agreement the less formal procedure would apply and the Bureau would be bound to pay the award of the arbitrator (subject to the procedure laid down).

In *White* v *London Transport Executive* [1971] 2 QB 721, [1971] 3 All ER 1, [1971] 3 WLR 169, Mrs White was injured when she was a passenger in a London Transport bus. She claimed under the 1969 Agreement on the basis that London Transport blamed a van driver — untraced — who had cut sharply in front of the bus, causing the bus driver to brake violently.

The Motor Insurers' Bureau, under the 1969 Agreement, required Mrs White to take proceedings against London Transport. The Bureau applied under O. 15, r. 6 to be joined as a party. The Master made the order sought and Waller J upheld the Master's order. The Court of Appeal took the view that, as the Bureau was standing behind the plaintiff in requiring her to bring proceedings against London Transport, it could not at the same time, as a party in the proceedings, cross-examine the plaintiff in an endeavour to show that her claim was excessive and that she was guilty of contributory negligence, as well as being in a position to cross-examine the Defendant's (London Transport's) witness. The joinder of the Motor Insurers' Bureau as a party was not, in the circumstances, considered 'necessary' within the terms of the rule. The action could be well and truly contested and adjudicated on as it was constituted. (It should be noted that this was a test case since 64 proceedings against London Transport and 260 proceedings elsewhere in the country had been instituted and were awaiting the decision in this case.)

It may well be that, on different facts and in different cases, the *discretion* allowed to the court to add parties might be exercised in favour of the Bureau, but such a course seems unlikely.

In *O'Neill* v *O'Brien and Another, The Times*, 21 March 1997 the Court of Appeal set aside a judgment to enable a plaintiff to start fresh proceedings for the purpose of involving the Bureau under the Uninsured Drivers Agreement 1988 when it had taken the view that it had not been informed of the date when damages were assessed by the Court.

The status of the Bureau since 1 October 1999 is now governed by clause 14 the Uninsured Drivers Agreement. The Bureau may now require a Claimant to consent to it being joined as a party as a condition for accepting liability to pay the claim.

10.   Untraced driver's negligence causing accident

The case of *Adams* v *Andrews* [1964] 2 Lloyds Rep 347 illustrates how the courts have taken into account the practice of the Bureau although it was not a party to the action and was not represented or heard. It also illustrates how the court's decision influenced the extensions and amendments of the remedies provided by the 1946 Agreement as incorporated in the 1969 and 1972 Agreements.

A teenage girl sustained serious brain injuries arising out of an accident that occurred while she was a passenger in a motor car driven by a friend. Although the friend's insurance policy would have covered passengers, his insurers repudiated his cover on the basis that he had been convicted of an offence in connection with the unroadworthiness of his tyres. (However, they made a small *ex gratia* payment to the girl.) The girl then sued the driver personally. He pleaded by way of defence that the accident was caused by the negligence of a motor cyclist travelling in the opposite direction. The motor cyclist was untraced.

Before the case was due to be heard, an approach was made by the solicitors for the girl to the Motor Insurers' Bureau, inviting it to give 'sympathetic consideration' to the claim, under Note 6 of the Notes annexed to the 1946 Motor Insurers' Bureau Agreement. The reply of the Bureau was it could and would do so only if, at the hearing of the case against the driver of the motor car, he was held to be without liability and the oncoming motor cyclist was held to be one hundred per cent liable for the accident. This meant that the case against the motorist friend had to be fought with what the judge described as 'a lack of cutting edge in the conduct of the case' and inviting the court to find that the untraced motor cyclist (not a party to the action and not represented) was entirely to blame.

At the hearing before Sachs J, the Defendant was held to be free from blame and the judge found the untraced motor cyclist to be entirely to blame for the accident. He found that, if he had awarded damages, they would have been assessed at £15,000. He then read Note 6 of the 1946 Agreement and added:

> Had the finding shown that the motor cyclist was three-quarters to blame and the Defendant one-quarter to blame, the result would have been a judgment against Mr Andrews for the full £15,000. Had there been such a finding, Mr Andrews would have been financially ruined, as he was not insured against accidents to passengers. Secondly, because of that insurance position, Miss Adams would probably receive little of the £15,000. Thirdly, the Motor Insurers' Bureau — who might now take an interest in the case — would not have even considered making an *ex gratia* payment to Miss Adams. There could hardly then have been a more striking series of miscarriages of justice.

He went on to say the discretion vested in an 'un-named and unappealable' body, the Bureau, was absolute and that the situation was as 'illogical as it was unjust'. He expressed the view that:

> ... in cases where the liability of a driver is under the Road Traffic Acts 'required to be covered by a policy of insurance' either the driver of the hit-and-run car is insured as by law required — in which case one

of the member companies of the Bureau would normally have to pay any damages awarded by the court, or else he is not insured, in which case the Bureau would likewise have to pay if he had been found, and judgment entered against him. That the injured person cannot recover as of right merely because he or she cannot secure a judgment as the driver has successfully evaded identification is lamentable and should not obtain ... He who has to go cap-in-hand for an *ex gratia* payment is always at a disadvantage ... There seems to be an immediate need so to revise the agreement with the Motor Insurers' Bureau that it cannot in law decline liabilities which should, in justice, be met by it in hit-and-run cases.

He went on to indicate that something should be done, either by legislation or by an amendment or extension of the Motor Insurers' Bureau Agreement, so that it could not decline liability for making payment in hit and run cases or because motorists or other persons who, at that time, were under no legal duty to insure against certain risks (such as injuries to their own passengers), were partly to blame.

The learned judge directed the solicitors acting for Miss Adams to refer the matter to the Bureau and report back to him. The Bureau investigated the case independently and came to the conclusion that no payment should be made to Miss Adams on an *ex gratia* basis under Note 6 annexed to the 1946 Agreement.

Following expressions of concern about this case, and about the adequacy of the Motor Insurers' Bureau scheme, at Parliamentary level, the Bureau made an *ex gratia* payment of £10,000 to Miss Adams, but made no contribution to her costs. The concern which arose from the case led eventually to an extension of protection afforded by the 1969 Agreement to victims of hit and run accidents.

11.   No appeal to court from Bureau's decisions

In *Persson* v *London Country Buses and Another* [1974] 1 All ER 1251, [1974] 1 WLR 569, 118 SJ 134, the Bureau decided to make no award to a Claimant on the basis that the untraced motorist would not, on the balance of probabilities, be liable to pay him damages.

Instead of making use of the appeal procedure laid down in the Agreement relating to untraced motorists (under clause 11), the Claimant decided to issue proceedings against the Bureau alleging that it had failed to pay him compensation in accordance with the terms of the Agreement.

The Bureau applied successfully to the Registrar (now described as a District Judge) to strike out the particulars of claim on the basis that it disclosed no cause of action. Judge Ruttle upheld the Registrar's decision and the Claimant's appeal to the Court of Appeal was in turn dismissed.

In any event it would seem that, as the Claimant was not a party to the Agreement, he would have no cause of action against the Bureau. The only person entitled to sue would possibly be the then Secretary of State for the Environment under the terms of the Agreement; but he is not known to have done so.

Cooper v *Motor Insurers' Bureau* [1985] QB 575, [1985] 1 All ER 449, [1985] 2 WLR 248 turned on a narrow point on the construction of ss. 143 and 145 Road Traffic Act 1972. The Court of Appeal did not accept that s. 143 extended the scope of compulsory insurance cover beyond 'others' (i.e., other than the driver) sustaining personal injuries. In other words, the sections did not cover injury to the *driver* of a motor cycle in a claim against its owner, on the failure of the brakes while testing it, resulting in the *driver* suffering complete tetraplegia. The Bureau was not liable under the 1972 Agreement relating to uninsured drivers to satisfy the judgment obtained against the *owner*.

The remaining question — whether the Bureau had waived its right to be given notice — did not fall to be decided in the case, although the deputy judge at first instance indicated that, had he found in favour of the plaintiff, he was satisfied on the evidence that the Bureau had not waived such notice.

In *Porter* v *Addo*; *Porter* v *Motor Insurers' Bureau* (1978) RTR 503, 122 SJ 592, Mrs Porter had bought a Volkswagen car in Holland, originally intending to ship it to Nigeria. It turned out that she could not afford to do that and she brought it to England. The customs officer at Harwich told her that she could not drive the car as she was not insured but that she should have it driven away by an insured driver.

The caretaker of the flat where she lived, Mr Addo, was known by Mrs Porter to drive a Hillman. She told him what had happened and he volunteered to drive the car to London. She assumed that he was covered by insurance to drive the car. It turned out that this assumption was incorrect.

An accident occurred on the journey between Harwich and London. Mrs Porter was seriously injured and was awarded £4,900 damages against Mr Addo.

The Motor Insurers' Bureau relied on clause 6(1)(c)(ii) of the 1972 Agreement relating to uninsured drivers.

Forbes J pointed out that the words in the subclause did not say 'having reason to believe' that there was no contract of insurance in force. The words were referable to a rational process of thought which was different from 'having a reasonable belief', a reference to the 'man on the Clapham omnibus'. Furthermore, the words did not say 'having no reason to believe that there was a contract in force'. The words fell to be construed as they stood.

On the basis that Mrs Porter had made it clear to Mr Addo that she needed an insured driver, she was entitled to assume by his assurance that he was an insured driver when he offered to help. There was nothing that should have caused her to 'believe that no such contract was in force'.

The approach of the civil court, it may be noted, differs from that adopted by the criminal courts with regard to the offences connected with driving while uninsured. The criminal courts are obliged to treat such offences as serious under s. 143 Road Traffic Act 1972 which makes them absolute offences.

12.   Meaning of 'motor vehicle'

Although there are no reported cases directly involving the Bureau relating to the meaning of a 'motor vehicle', there are many criminal cases in which the matter has been considered. The expression 'motor vehicle' is defined in s. 185(1) of the Road Traffic Act 1988 as 'a mechanically propelled vehicle intended or adapted for use on roads'. The test adopted in *Chief Constable of Avon and Somerset* v *Fleming* [1987] 1 All ER 318 QBD was whether a reasonable person, looking at the vehicle, would say that its general use encompassed possible general road use. The *particular* use of the vehicle is considered to be irrelevant. In *Fleming*, a motor cycle had been adapted for use in the sport of 'scrambling' on private land by removal of its registration plate, reflector, lights and speedometer. The magistrates' court was held entitled to find that the description by the police of the vehicle was vague and unsatisfactory and that the prosecution had not proved that the motor cycle (or what remained of it) was a motor vehicle.

In *Burns* v *Currell* [1963] 2 All ER 297 QBD, a go-kart was regarded as not falling within the definition of 'motor vehicle'. The vehicle had an engine at the rear, with a tubular frame mounted on four small wheels, was equipped with a single seat, steering wheel and column and an efficient silencer. Its brakes operated on the rear wheels only. It had no horn, springs, parking brake, driving mirror or wings. There was evidence before the court that it had been used on the road on only one occasion. There was no evidence that other go-karts were used on the road. Again the Divisional Court applied a test involving a matter-of-fact jury approach: 'There was not sufficient evidence ... to prove beyond a reasonable doubt that any *reasonable person* [author's italics] looking at the go-kart would say that one of its uses would be a use on the road nor that it was fit or apt for use on the road although it was capable of full use.'

Another way of approaching the same problem was expressed in *Daley and Others* v *Hargreaves* [1961] 1 All ER 552 by Salmon J, who suggested that the word 'intended' in the definition might be paraphrased as 'suitable or apt'. The court in *Daley* considered whether or not a dumper was within the definition of a motor vehicle. It reached the conclusion that there was no evidence to show that the dumpers in question were 'intended' or adapted for use on roads.

As each case must turn on its own facts on the evidence before the court, so the Bureau will consider each case on its own facts.

13.   More than one cause of accident

Many accidents have more than one cause. *Rouse* v *Squires and Others* [1973] 2 All ER 903 is one example. An articulated lorry skidded on the frosty surface of a motorway, due to the driver's negligent driving. After jack-knifing, the lorry ended up blocking the first and second lanes of the motorway. A car travelling behind, after colliding with the lorry, left its rear lights on. A second lorry driver, realising what had happened, drove his lorry safely past. After parking, he returned to render assistance. A third lorry pulled up fifteen feet away from the broken-down lorry and left his headlights on to illuminate the broken-down lorry and warn other drivers of the situation. The driver of a fourth lorry, driving at high speed, did not realise, at 400 yards' distance, that the vehicles were stationary or that two lanes of the motorway were obstructed. When 150 yards away, he applied his brakes and skidded on the frosty surface. His lorry collided with the second lorry, pushing it forward, knocking its driver down, and causing his death. The widow was awarded damages against the driver of the fourth lorry for his negligent driving. He claimed contribution against the first lorry driver and his employers in respect of the initial negligence. The Court of Appeal held that the first lorry driver contributed to the causation of the accident although the *immediate* cause was the negligent driving of the vehicle colliding with it or with some other vehicle or person. A grave danger on the highway had been brought about by the initial negligent driving. The danger was reduced by the illumination provided by the headlights, but it had continued up to the moment of the collision and had been a factor in causing the collision. At p. 911, MacKenna J said:

> Where the party guilty of the prior negligence has created a dangerous situation, and the danger is still continuing to a substantial degree at the time of the accident, and the accident would not have happened but for this continuing danger, he is responsible for the accident as well as the party who was subsequently negligent.

14.   Arbitrator may award interest

In *Evans* v *Motor Insurers' Bureau, The Times*, 10 November 1997, Thomas J, in the Commercial Court of the Queen's Bench Division held that where the Bureau had made an award subsequently found to be inappropriate by the Arbitrator, interest could be awarded by the Arbitrator in the exercise of his or her discretion in two types of case. One would be on the basis that the victim should be compensated for the delay between the dates of the Bureau's and the Arbitrator's decisions. The other was when the Bureau had not acted with reasonable expedition, in which event interest could be awarded to cover the period beween the date the sum ought to have been paid and the date of the Arbitrator's award.

It is understood that the judgment in this case has been made the subject of a 'Francovitch' claim against the Government. Such a claim arises when a Member State funds to implement a Directive of the European Community. (See *Francovitch* v *Italian Republic* C6 and 9/90 ECR I–5337.)

15.   No compensation to passenger knowing driver uninsured

In *Stinton* v *Stinton* [1995] RTR 157 (Court of Appeal), the Defendant driver bought a car the afternoon before the accident. Both driver and injured passenger were drunk. On the facts of the case, as found, the passenger knew that the driver was uninsured. It had become the 'common object' of the two to embark on a long night's drinking with the passenger driven around uninsured. The Bureau was entitled to exemption from liability under Clause 6 of the then current Uninsured Drivers Agreement. The passenger's claim failed on the basis that he was involved in a 'joint enterprise' with the driver and, as such was a 'person using the vehicle' within the clause.

Since 1 October 1999, the burden of proof in such a case would be on the Bureau, subject to the items set out in clause 6(3) of the 1999 Uninsured Drivers Agreement. Similar remarks would apply in such circumstances as outlined in the next case.

16. Pillion passenger entitled to compensation

In *Hatton* v *Hall* (1996) *The Times*, 15 May 1996 (Court of Appeal) the Court considered and distinguished the *Stinton* Case (see **15** above) on the basis that not all plans shared between driver and passenger gave the passenger sufficient management of the vehicle to make him a 'person using the vehicle'. A more restricted meaning of the verb 'using' was applied to the facts of this particular case, the pillion passenger having been driven on a 10 mile journey to a public house.

Incidentally, it may be of interest to insurance companies and those advising them that the European Court in *Criminal Proceedings against Bernaldez* (Case C 129/94) European Law Report, Luxembourg 6 May 1996 it was held *not* to be contrary to Council Directive 72/166/EEC of 24 April 1972 in European Law for an insurer to have the right, in a contract of insurance, to recover against an insured driver any payment it has been obliged to make in respect of damage caused to a third party by his drunken driving.

Eight

The Claims Procedure

1. Introduction

Payments by the Bureau's central fund since 1946 total some £970 million, excluding payments made direct to Claimants on behalf of the Bureau (see below). Payments are likely to reach in excess of £200 million per annum. Many Claimants are under the mistaken impression that the Bureau takes an adversarial attitude to claims. This is reflected in the expression 'claims *against*' the Bureau; they should more accurately be described as claims *on* the Bureau, similar to compensation claims under various statutory provisions. The Bureau was set up to fulfil, not to avoid, the obligations within its terms of reference. These include making payments where appropriate and not making undue use of reasons not to pay. It therefore seeks to co-operate with solicitors and other representatives of Claimants, and to work with them constructively in carrying out the terms of the Agreements, for the benefit of applicants entitled to awards and payments.

2. Delegating to the insurers

When a claim is made on the Motor Insurers' Bureau, the Bureau delegates the investigation to one of its members *as agent*. If the claim relates to an uninsured motorist, the delegated member is authorised to go as far as settling it. If the claim relates to an untraced driver, the delegated member insurer (except in those cases where the 'accelerated procedure' applies — see p. 17) investigates and then submits an objective report for consideration by the Bureau to assist in reaching a decision.

Where there is an insurance policy in existence, the insurance company or Lloyd's syndicate which granted it will deal with the claim and the Bureau will not be concerned. Under the domestic agreement certain obligations of the Bureau are discharged by the insurers even though the insurance cover was inoperative in the circumstances of the particular accident giving rise to the claim. This acceptance of responsibility on behalf of the Bureau is based on the fact that members of the Bureau are required to make certain payments into the fund administered by the Bureau and in the long run it matters little or nothing that the insurance companies concerned pay directly out of their own funds instead of contributing towards the additional amount which would be required were payment made by the Bureau.

3. Inquiries as to insurance cover

Before notifying the Bureau of a claim where it is believed that there is no insurance cover, full and proper inquiries should be made. It may be quicker (and indeed cheaper) in the general run of cases, if there is no reply from a proposed Defendant to a claim arising out of an accident, to incur the expense of engaging a local solicitor or inquiry agent to call on the proposed Defendant with a view to obtaining details of his insurers, if any. Only if the inquiries reveal that there was no insurance cover, the Bureau should be notified and the full facts placed before it so that time and energy may be saved in its own investigations.

It should be noted that the provisions of s. 151 of the Road Traffic Act 1988 will protect a Claimant if the appropriate notice is given to the Defendant's insurers (see pp. 27 and 28). It should also be borne in mind that some delay takes place by reason of investigation by the Bureau or the insurance company delegated to investigate the case on its behalf. In some cases where it is suspected that a policy is in existence but details are not known, the Bureau refers to the head offices of the insurers thought to be concerned and some delay may take place while the head office endeavours to trace the policy with its particular branch.

4. Insurance company in liquidation

Where an insurance company goes into liquidation (and there have unfortunately been more than a few such cases), it takes a little time for a liquidator to be appointed and for an agreement to be reached between the liquidator and the Bureau. Such agreement is necessary to protect the Bureau, as it then takes over the rights of the insurers against the insured under the terms of the particular policy.

On the liquidation of the Vehicle and General group of companies in 1970 arrangements were made as a 'one off' operation, it was hoped, by the then British Insurance Association (now the Association of British Insurers) for a fund to be set up to deal with claims for personal injuries which would normally have been dealt with by that group of companies. Claims were dealt with and investigated by the Bureau acting *as agents* for the Association. This normally involves a great deal of additional work for the Bureau. It is, however, assisted in that work by delegation of the investigation to claims officers of the insurance company members. Nevertheless, the investigation and reports so obtained have to be considered by the Bureau in reaching its decision.

The Association of British Insurers only pays claims where the Motor Insurers' Bureau is *not* normally liable. Where the Bureau is liable, the claims made are dealt with by the Bureau as *principal*.

5. General procedure

As noted on p. 4, notification of a claim is normally made initially by letter or phone call from the Claimant or from those representing him after which a form supplied by the Bureau should be completed, accompanied by the relevant documents and forwarded by the Claimant or those representing him. Further information is sought by the Bureau through its own efforts — for example, by inquiries of witnesses or experts, or by seeking the assistance of the Claimant or the Claimant's advisers. It should be noted that the Bureau is able to decide a claim only on the basis of the facts available to it.

This relative lack of formality should have the effect of encouraging Claimants to come forward and pursue the means available through the Motor Insurers' Bureau Agreements of obtaining compensation for injuries or damage to property.

Nine

Conclusions

1. Summary of achievements

Before looking forward to the future, it may be useful to look back to the recommendations of the Cassel Committee (see p. 2) to see how far the Bureau's work has filled the gaps left in road traffic legislation. The conclusion of the Committee that it was not feasible to provide for the victims of accidents caused by untraced motorists has been proved wrong. Under the 1946 Agreement, such victims had only the right to receive sympathetic consideration from the Bureau. Since the 1969 Agreement, the Bureau has an *obligation* to meet their claims. There is also now a right of appeal available to dissatisfied Claimants.

The recommendation of the Committee that a fund be set up to meet claims when an insurance company becomes insolvent has to some extent been implemented by the British Insurance Association (now the Association of British Insurers) in cases not involving the Bureau. The Bureau itself has dealt and will continue to deal 'as a second line of defence' with the other claims relating to uninsured and untraced motorists under the two current Agreements, as recommended by Cassel.

The fact that passenger insurance became compulsory from 1 December 1972 has plugged the largest gap in this area of the law. The Bureau has since then met claims which did not fall to be considered under the previous Agreements. As damage to property has to some extent become compulsorily insurable from 31 December 1988, a further gap has been filled.

2.   The future

There are only two possible remaining areas for consideration; one concerns claims arising from the use of motor vehicles other than on a public road; the other relates to claims where it is not certain that the accident was caused by a driver of a motor vehicle. The first is a matter of principle in respect of which there could be an extension of the scope of the Agreements. It should be remembered that the Motor Insurers' Bureau Agreements depend for the scope of their application on the extent of the legislative requirements for compulsory insurance. It would be necessary for a new Road Traffic Act to redefine 'road' for the Bureau to be liable. (It is understood that legislation is shortly to be introduced to clarify this point.) The second is one of practice. It is believed that the Bureau often meets such claims as those where a person is found injured at the side of a road, in spite of the fact that the evidence would probably not be sufficient to satisfy a court that the accident was caused by a motor vehicle.

3.   The Criminal Injuries Compensation Scheme

There is a connection between the work of the Bureau and that done under the Criminal Injuries Compensation Scheme in that information is exchanged about awards and other matters. Their activities to some extent overlap, but this overlap is kept to a minimum. It should be remembered that the Criminal Injuries Compensation Scheme deals with claims arising out of such criminal acts as fall within the ambit of its 'jurisdiction'. Thus a claim was excluded under para. 11 of the 1990 Criminal Injuries Compensation Scheme as the injury was 'attributable to traffic offences ... except where such injury is due to a deliberate attempt to run the victim down'. In *R v Criminal Injuries Compensation Board ex parte Neave and ex parte Marsden* 29 October 1997 (unreported), the victims' injuries were the subject of claims which were refused by the Motor Insurers' Bureau as the injuries were sustained other than on a *public* road. Claims then made under the 1990 Criminal Injuries Scheme were also refused based on the paragraph referred to.

For some years before November 1995 (when the *Neave* and *Marsden* claims were rejected) the Board had met similar claims either due to inconsistency or a wrong interpretation of the scheme, i.e., by regarding reckless driving as a crime of violence.

The wording of paragraph 11 has been replaced in the 1996 scheme to cover injury 'attributable to the deliberate use of a vehicle to inflict, or attempt to inflict, injury on any person'. If the claims of *Neave* and *Marsden* had arisen on a date when the 1996 scheme applied, they would probably have been successful.

Where the facts of any particular claim warrant it, claims should be notified both to the Motor Insurers' Bureau and under the Criminal Injuries Compensation Scheme, with a view to eventual resolution by one or the other. In a case brought to the attention of the author, a driver was forced off the road and sustained injuries. The other vehicle turned out to have been stolen and the driver disappeared. Although claims were made on the Bureau and under the Criminal Injuries Scheme, both unfortunately failed. The Bureau took the view that the act of forcing the victim's vehicle off the road was 'deliberate' and thus outside the scope of the Uninsured Drivers Agreement. After due consideration, when the claim was heard (by way of appeal), with oral evidence from the victim and a police officer who investigated, the Panel decided that it was not satisfied that 'the injury [was] attributable to the use of a vehicle ... deliberately to inflict, or attempt to inflict, injury' on the Claimant, under para. 11 of the Scheme. It is submitted that such ''borderline'' cases must be rather rare. There have been discussions from time to time between the Bureau and the Criminal Injuries Compensation Authority in an endeavour to clarify the scope of the Bureau's Agreements and the Criminal Injuries Compensation Scheme. Efforts are often made informally to ensure that, where appropriate, an innocent victim receives an award and does not 'fall between two stools'.

4. Periodic review

The author's personal view is that the Bureau is the appropriate body to continue to deal with cases within the scope of the current Agreements. It might, however, be convenient to review the scope and application of the Agreement at regular intervals, for example, every five years. This would mean that a summary of cases dealt with by the Bureau could be looked at either by the Secretary of State for Environment, Transport and the Regions or by an independent party nominated by him and the Bureau. He could then make recommendations, both for the possibility of extending the scope of the Agreements (for example, to include claims arising from incidents not taking place on a public highway — see pp. 36 to 40) and for streamlining the procedure adopted by the Bureau in dealing with claims.

One area which may be considered would be where a claim is made and there is some difficulty in reaching a decision e.g., as to a number of potential Defendants. Reference could be made to the Bureau for guidance and a suggested (and approved) course to be adopted i.e., to enter judgment against one Defendant who had not entered an appearance or to proceed to a full hearing against that Defendant and another Defendant who had entered an appearance and had served a defence. Under the current Uninsured Drivers Agreement such informal, or even formal, steps are likely to be taken.

5.   The Bureau as Defendant to proceedings

It had been suggested in earlier editions of this book that the Bureau should be allowed the possibility of being made a nominal Defendant (or Defender) in certain claims. This, of course, might be argued to assist the Bureau by permitting it to take advantage of any defence which would have been available to a Defendant. It would also assist the Claimant in having his case fully investigated in the normal course of litigation by a court of law. Such issues as contributory negligence could be decided judicially. It had, however, been pointed out that any such litigation would significantly increase the expense of the Bureau.

The Bureau has so far provided a relatively cheap, informal and effective way of dealing with claims which avoids, to a large extent, the necessity of such litigation. It has also been known to make awards on the basis of hearsay evidence or, occasionally, on little or no evidence. This would not occur if such evidence were to be weighed by the strict rules of evidence that would apply in claims heard by a court.

However, some progress has been made since the Uninsured Drivers Agreement came into effect for accidents occurring on or after 1 October 1999. Under clause 14 of this Agreement, a Claimant is obliged to consent to the Bureau being joined as a party to the proceedings if requested to do so by the Bureau. The Bureau is not liable under the Agreement to satisfy a judgment in favour of the Claimant unless this requirement is fulfilled.

It remains to be seen how the new Agreement works in practice with the added facility for the Bureau to be made a party to proceedings.

Appendices

Motor Insurers' Bureau (Compensation of Victims of Uninsured Drivers) Agreement 1999

THIS AGREEMENT is made the thirteenth day of August 1999 between the SECRETARY OF STATE FOR THE ENVIRONMENT, TRANSPORT AND THE REGIONS (hereinafter referred to as 'the Secretary of State') and the MOTOR INSURERS' BUREAU, whose registered office is at 152 Silbury Boulevard, Milton Keynes MK9 1NB (hereinafter referred to as 'MIB') and is SUPPLEMENTAL to an Agreement (hereinafter called 'the Principal Agreement') made the 31st Day of December 1945 between the Minister of War Transport and the insurers transacting compulsory motor insurance business in Great Britain by or on behalf of whom the said Agreement was signed and in pursuance of paragraph 1 of which MIB was incorporated.

IT IS HEREBY AGREED AS FOLLOWS—

INTERPRETATION

General definitions

1.   In this Agreement, unless the context otherwise requires, the following expressions have the following meanings—
    '1988 Act' means the Road Traffic Act 1988;
    '1988 Agreement' means the Agreement made on 21 December 1988 between the Secretary of State for Transport and MIB;
    'bank holiday' means a day which is, or is to be observed as, a bank holiday under the Banking and Financial Dealings Act 1971;

'claimant' means a person who has commenced or who proposes to commence relevant proceedings and has made an application under this Agreement in respect thereof;

'contract of insurance' means a policy of insurance or a security covering a relevant liability;

'insurer' includes the giver of a security;

'MIB's obligation' means the obligation contained in clause 5;

'property' means any property whether real, heritable or personal;

'relevant liability' means a liability in respect of which a contract of insurance must be in force to comply with Part VI of the 1988 Act;

'relevant proceedings' means proceedings in respect of a relevant liability (and 'commencement', in relation to such proceedings means, in England and Wales, the date on which a Claim Form or other originating process is issued by a Court or, in Scotland, the date on which the originating process is served on the Defender)

'relevant sum' means a sum payable or remaining payable under an unsatisfied judgment, including—

(a) an amount payable or remaining payable in respect of interest on that sum, and

(b) either the whole of the costs (whether taxed or not) awarded by the Court as part of that judgment or, where the judgment includes an award in respect of a liability which is not a relevant liability, such proportion of those costs as the relevant liability bears to the total sum awarded under the judgment;

'specified excess' means £300 or such other sum as may from time to time be agreed in writing between the Secretary of State and MIB;

'unsatisfied judgment' means a judgment or order (by whatever name called) in respect of a relevant liability which has not been satisfied in full within seven days from the date upon which the claimant became entitled to enforce it.

Meaning of references

2.—(1) Save as otherwise herein provided, the Interpretation Act 1978 shall apply for the interpretation of this Agreement as it applies for the interpretation of an Act of Parliament.

(2) Where, under this Agreement, something is required to be done—

(a) within a specified period after or from the happening of a particular event, the period begins on the day after the happening of that event;

(b) within or not less than a specified period before a particular event, the period ends on the day immediately before the happening of that event.

(3) Where, apart from this paragraph, the period in question, being a period of seven days or less, would include a Saturday, Sunday or bank holiday or Christmas Day or Good Friday, that day shall be excluded.

(4) Save where expressly otherwise provided, a reference in this Agreement to a numbered clause is a reference to the clause bearing that number in this Agreement and a reference to a numbered paragraph is a reference to a paragraph bearing that number in the clause in which the reference occurs.

(5)   In this Agreement—
(a)   a reference (however framed) to the doing of any act or thing by or the happening of any event in relation to the claimant includes a reference to the doing of that act or thing by or the happening of that event in relation to a Solicitor or other person acting on his behalf, and
(b)   a requirement to give notice to, or to serve documents upon, MIB or an insurer mentioned in clause 9(1)(a) shall be satisfied by the giving of the notice to, or the service of the documents upon, a Solicitor acting on its behalf in the manner provided for.

Claimants not of full age or capacity

3.   Where, under and in accordance with this Agreement—
(a)   any act or thing is done to or by a Solicitor or other person acting on behalf of a claimant,
(b)   any decision is made by or in respect of a Solicitor or other person acting on behalf of a claimant, or
(c)   any sum is paid to a Solicitor or other person acting on behalf of a claimant,
then, whatever may be the age or other circumstances affecting the capacity of the claimant, that act, thing, decision or sum shall be treated as if it had been done to or by, or made in respect of or paid to a claimant of full age and capacity.

PRINCIPAL TERMS

Duration of Agreement

4.—(1)   This Agreement shall come into force on 1st October 1999 in relation to accidents occurring on or after that date and, save as provided by clause 23, the 1988 Agreement shall cease and determine immediately before that date.
(2)   This Agreement may be determined by the Secretary of State or by MIB giving to the other not less than twelve months' notice in writing but without prejudice to its continued operation in respect of accidents occurring before the date of termination.

MIB's obligation to satisfy compensation claims

5.—(1)   Subject to clauses 6 to 17, if a claimant has obtained against any person in a Court in Great Britain a judgment which is an unsatisfied judgment then MIB will pay the relevant sum to, or to the satisfaction of, the claimant or will cause the same to be so paid.
(2)   Paragraph (1) applies whether or not the person liable to satisfy the judgment is in fact covered by a contract of insurance and whatever may be the cause of his failure to satisfy the judgment.

EXCEPTIONS TO AGREEMENT

6.—(1)   Clause 5 does not apply in the case of an application made in respect of a claim of any of the following descriptions (and, where part only of a claim satisfies such a description, clause 5 does not apply to that part)—

(a)   a claim arising out of a relevant liability incurred by the user of a vehicle owned by or in the possession of the Crown, unless—

(i)   responsibility for the existence of a contract of insurance under Part VI of the 1988 Act in relation to that vehicle had been undertaken by some other person (whether or not the person liable was in fact covered by a contract of insurance), or

(ii)   the relevant liability was in fact covered by a contract of insurance;

(b)   a claim arising out of the use of a vehicle which is not required to be covered by a contract of insurance by virtue of section 144 of the 1988 Act, unless the use is in fact covered by such a contract;

(c)   a claim by, or for the benefit of, a person ('the beneficiary') other than the person suffering death, injury or other damage which is made either—

(i)   in respect of a cause of action or a judgment which has been assigned to the beneficiary, or

(ii)   pursuant to a right of subrogation or contractual or other right belonging to the beneficiary;

(d)   a claim in respect of damage to a motor vehicle or losses arising therefrom where, at the time when the damage to it was sustained—

(i)   there was not in force in relation to the use of that vehicle such a contract of insurance as is required by Part VI of the 1988 Act, and

(ii)   the claimant either knew or ought to have known that that was the case;

(e)   a claim which is made in respect of a relevant liability described in paragraph (2) by a claimant who, at the time of the use giving rise to the relevant liability was voluntarily allowing himself to be carried in the vehicle and, either before the commencement of his journey in the vehicle or after such commencement if he could reasonably be expected to have alighted from it, knew or ought to have known that—

(i)   the vehicle had been stolen or unlawfully taken,

(ii)   the vehicle was being used without there being in force in relation to its use such a contract of insurance as would comply with Part VI of the 1988 Act,

(iii)   the vehicle was being used in the course or furtherance of a crime, or

(iv)   the vehicle was being used as a means of escape from, or avoidance of, lawful apprehension.

(2)   The relevant liability referred to in paragraph (1)(e) is a liability incurred by the owner or registered keeper or a person using the vehicle in which the claimant was being carried.

(3)   The burden of proving that the claimant knew or ought to have known of any matter set out in paragraph (1)(e) shall be on MIB but, in the absence of evidence to the contrary, proof by MIB of any of the following matters shall be

taken as proof of the claimant's knowledge of the matter set out in paragraph (1)(e)(ii)—

(a)   that the claimant was the owner or registered keeper of the vehicle or had caused or permitted its use;

(b)   that the claimant knew the vehicle was being used by a person who was below the minimum age at which he could be granted a licence authorising the driving of a vehicle of that class.

(c)   that the claimant knew that the person driving the vehicle was disqualified for holding or obtaining a driving licence;

(d)   that the claimant knew that the user of the vehicle was neither its owner nor registered keeper nor an employee of the owner or registered keeper nor the owner or registered keeper of any other vehicle.

(4)   Knowledge which the claimant has or ought to have for the purposes of paragraph (1)(e) includes knowledge of matters which he could reasonably be expected to have been aware of had he not been under the self-induced influence of drink or drugs.

(5)   For the purposes of this clause—

(a)   a vehicle which has been unlawfully removed from the possession of the Crown shall be taken to continue in that possession whilst it is kept so removed,

(b)   references to a person being carried in a vehicle include references to his being carried upon, entering, getting on to and alighting from the vehicle, and

(c)   'owner', in relation to a vehicle which is the subject of a hiring agreement or a hire-purchase agreement, means the person in possession of the vehicle under that agreement.

CONDITIONS PRECEDENT TO MIB'S OBLIGATION

Form of application

7.—(1)   MIB shall incur no liability under MIB's obligation unless an application is made to the person specified in clause 9(1)—

(a)   in such form

(b)   giving such information about the relevant proceedings and other matters relevant to this Agreement, and

(c)   accompanied by such documents as MIB may reasonably require.

(2)   Where an application is signed by a person who is neither the claimant nor a Solicitor acting on his behalf MIB may refuse to accept the application (and shall incur no liability under MIB's obligation) until it is reasonably satisfied that, having regard to the status of the signatory and his relationship to the claimant, the claimant is fully aware of the contents and effect of the application but subject thereto MIB shall not refuse to accept such an application by reason only that it is signed by a person other than the claimant or his Solicitor.

Service of notices etc.

8.   Any notice required to be given or documents to be supplied to MIB pursuant to clauses 9 to 12 of this Agreement shall be sufficiently given or

supplied only if sent by facsimile transmission or by Registered or Recorded Delivery post to MIB's registered office for the time being and delivery shall be proved by the production of a facsimile transmission report produced by the sender's facsimile machine or an appropriate postal receipt.

Notice of relevant proceedings

9.—(1)   MIB shall incur no liability under MIB's obligation unless proper notice of the bringing of the relevant proceedings has been given by the claimant not later than fourteen days after the commencement of those proceedings—

(a)   in the case of proceedings in respect of a relevant liability which is covered by a contract of insurance with an insurer whose identity can be ascertained, to that insurer;

(b)   in any other case, to MIB.

(2)   In this clause 'proper notice' means, except in so far as any part of such information or any copy document or other thing has already been supplied under clause 7—

(a)   notice in writing that proceedings have been commenced by Claim Form, Writ, or other means,

(b)   a copy of the sealed Claim Form, Writ or other official document providing evidence of the commencement of the proceedings and, in Scotland, a statement of the means of service,

(c)   a copy or details of any insurance policy providing benefits in the case of the death, bodily injury or damage to property to which the proceedings relate where the claimant is the insured party and the benefits are available to him,

(d)   copies of all correspondence in the possession of the claimant or (as the case may be) his Solicitor or agent to or from the Defendant or the Defender or (as the case may be) his Solicitor, insurers or agent which is relevant to—

(i)   the death, bodily injury or damage for which the Defendant or Defender is alleged to be responsible, or

(ii)   any contract of insurance which covers, or which may or has been alleged to cover, liability for such death, injury or damage the benefit of which is, or is claimed to be, available to Defendant or Defender,

(e)   subject to paragraph (3), a copy of the Particulars of Claim whether or not indorsed on the Claim Form, Writ or other originating process, and whether or not served (in England and Wales) on any Defendant or (in Scotland) on any Defender, and

(f)   a copy of all other documents which are required under the appropriate rules of procedure to be served on a Defendant or Defender with the Claim Form, Writ or other originating process or with the Particulars of Claim,

(g)   such other information about the relevant proceedings as MIB may reasonably specify.

(3)   If, in the case of proceedings commenced in England or Wales, the Particulars of Claim (including any document required to be served therewith) has not yet been served with the Claim Form or other originating process paragraph (2)(e) shall be sufficiently complied with if a copy thereof is served on MIB not later than seven days after it is served on the Defendant.

Notice of service of proceedings

10.—(1) This clause applies where the relevant proceedings are commenced in England or Wales.

(2) MIB shall incur no liability under MIB's obligation unless the claimant has, not later than the appropriate date, given notice in writing to the person specified in clause 9(1) of the date of service of the Claim Form or other originating process in the relevant proceedings.

(3) In this clause, 'the appropriate date' means the day falling—

(a) seven days after—

(i) the date when the claimant receives notification from the Court that service of the Claim Form or other originating process has occurred,

(ii) the date when the claimant receives notification from the Defendant that service of the Claim Form or other originating process has occurred, or

(iii) the date of personal service, or

(b) fourteen days after the date when service is deemed to have occurred in accordance with the Civil Procedure Rules,

whichever of those days occurs first.

Further information

11.—(1) MIB shall incur no liability under MIB's obligation unless the claimant has, not later than seven days after the occurrence of any of the following events, namely—

(a) the filing of a defence in the relevant proceedings,

(b) any amendment to the Particulars of Claim or any amendment of or addition to any schedule or other document required to be served therewith, and

(c) either—

(i) the setting down of the case for trial, or

(ii) where the court gives notice to the claimant of the trial date, the date when that notice is received,

given notice in writing of the date of that event to the person specified in clause 9(1) and has, in the case of the filing of a defence or an amendment of the Particulars of Claim or any amendment of or addition to any schedule or other document required to be served therewith, supplied a copy thereof to that person.

(2) MIB shall incur no liability under MIB's obligation unless the claimant furnishes to the person specified in clause 9(1) within a reasonable time after being required to do so such further information and documents in support of his claim as MIB may reasonably require notwithstanding that the claimant may have complied with clause 7(1).

Notice of intention to apply for judgment

12.—(1) MIB shall incur no liability under MIB's obligation unless the claimant has, after commencement of the relevant proceedings and not less than thirty-five days before the appropriate date, given notice in writing to the person specified in clause 9(1) of his intention to apply for or to sign judgment in the relevant proceedings.

(2)   In this clause, 'the appropriate date' means the date when the application for judgment is made or, as the case may be, the signing of judgment occurs.

Section 154 of the 1988 Act

13.   MIB shall incur no liability under MIB's obligation unless the claimant has as soon as reasonably practicable—

(a)   demanded the information and, where appropriate, the particulars specified in section 154(1) of the 1988 Act, and

(b)   if the person of whom the demand is made fails to comply with the provisions of that subsection—

(i)   made a formal complaint to a police officer in respect of such failure, and

(ii)   used all reasonable endeavours to obtain the name and address of the registered keeper of the vehicle.

or, if so required by MIB, has authorised MIB to take such steps on his behalf.

Prosecution of proceedings

14.   MIB shall incur no liability under MIB's obligation—

(a)   unless the claimant has, if so required by MIB and having been granted a full indemnity by MIB as to costs, taken all reasonable steps to obtain judgment against every person who may be liable (including any person who may be vicariously liable) in respect of the injury or death or damage to property, or

(b)   if the claimant, upon being requested to do so by MIB, refuses to consent to MIB being joined as a party to the relevant proceedings.

Assignment of judgment and undertakings

15.   MIB shall incur no liability under MIB's obligation unless the claimant has—

(a)   assigned to MIB or its nominee the unsatisfied judgment, whether or not that judgment includes an amount in respect of a liability other than a relevant liability, and any order for costs made in the relevant proceedings, and

(b)   undertaken to repay to MIB any sum paid to him—

(i)   by MIB in discharge of MIB's obligation if the judgment is subsequently set aside either as a whole or in respect of the part of the relevant liability to which that sum relates;

(ii)   by any other person by way of compensation or benefit for the death, bodily injury or other damage to which the relevant proceedings relate, including a sum which would have been deductible under the provisions of clause 17 if it had been received before MIB was obliged to satisfy MIB's obligation.

LIMITATIONS ON MIB's LIABILITY

Compensation for damage to property

16.—(1)   Where a claim under this Agreement includes a claim in respect of damage to property, MIB's obligation in respect of that part of the relevant sum which is awarded for such damage and any losses arising therefrom (referred to in this clause as 'the property damage compensation') is limited in accordance with the following paragraphs.

(2)   Where the property damage compensation does not exceed the specified excess, MIB shall incur no liability.

(3)   Where the property damage compensation in respect of any one accident exceeds the specified excess but does not exceed £250,000, MIB shall incur liability only in respect of the property damage compensation less the specified excess.

(4)   Where the property damage compensation in respect of any one accident exceeds £250,000, MIB shall incur liability only in respect of the sum of £250,000 less the specified excess.

Compensation received from other sources

17.   Where a claimant has received compensation from—

(a)   the Policyholders Protection Board under the Policyholders Protection Act 1975, or

(b)   an insurer under an insurance agreement or arrangement, or

(c)   any other source,

in respect of the death, bodily injury or other damage to which the relevant proceedings relate and such compensation has not been taken into account in the calculation of the relevant sum MIB may deduct from the relevant sum, in addition to any sum deductible under clause 16, an amount equal to that compensation.

MISCELLANEOUS

Notifications of decisions by MIB

18.   Where a claimant—

(a)   has made an application in accordance with clause 7, and

(b)   has given to the person specified in clause 9(1) proper notice of the relevant proceedings in accordance with clause 9(2),

MIB shall—

(i)   give a reasoned reply to any request made by the claimant relating to the payment of compensation in pursuance of MIB's obligation, and

(ii)   as soon as reasonably practicable notify the claimant in writing of its decision regarding the payment of the relevant sum, together with the reasons for that decision.

Reference of disputes to the Secretary of State

19.—(1)   In the event of any dispute as to the reasonableness of a requirement made by MIB for the supply of information or documentation or for the taking of any step by the claimant, it may be referred by the claimant or MIB to the Secretary of State whose decision shall be final.

(2)   Where a dispute is referred to the Secretary of State—

(a)   MIB shall supply the Secretary of State and, if it has not already done so, the claimant with notice in writing of the requirement from which the dispute arises, together with the reasons for that requirement and such further information as MIB considers relevant, and

(b)   where the dispute is referred by the claimant, the claimant shall supply the Secretary of State and, if he has not already done so, MIB with notice in writing of the grounds on which he disputes the reasonableness of the requirement.

Recoveries

20.   Nothing in this Agreement shall prevent an insurer from providing by conditions in a contract of insurance that all sums paid by the insurer or by MIB by virtue of the Principal Agreement or this Agreement in or towards the discharge of the liability of the insured shall be recoverable by them or by MIB from the insured or from any other person.

Apportionment of damages, etc.

21.—(1)   Where an unsatisfied judgment which includes an amount in respect of a liability other than a relevant liability has been assigned to MIB or its nominee in pursuance of clause 15 MIB shall—

(a)   apportion any sum it receives in satisfaction or partial satisfaction of the judgment according to the proportion which the damages awarded in respect of the relevant liability bear to the damages awarded in respect of the other liability, and

(b)   account to the claimant in respect of the moneys received properly apportionable to the other liability.

(2)   Where the sum received includes an amount in respect of interest or an amount awarded under an order for costs, the interest or the amount received in pursuance of the order shall be dealt with in the manner provided in paragraph (1).

Agents

22.   MIB may perform any of its obligations under this Agreement by agents.

Transitional provisions

23.—(1)   The 1988 Agreement shall continue in force in relation to claims arising out of accidents occurring before 1st October 1999 with the modifications contained in paragraph (2).

(2)   In relation to any claim made under the 1988 Agreement after this Agreement has come into force, the 1988 Agreement shall apply as if there were inserted after clause 6 thereof—

'6A.   Where any person in whose favour a judgment in respect of a relevant liability has been made has
    (a)   made a claim under this Agreement, and
    (b)   satisfied the requirements specified in clause 5 hereof,
MIB shall, if requested to do so, give him a reasoned reply regarding the satisfaction of that claim.'.

IN WITNESS whereof the Secretary of State has caused his Corporate Seal to be hereunto affixed and the Motor Insurers' Bureau has caused its Common Seal to be hereunto affixed the day and year first above written.

THE   CORPORATE   SEAL   of   the   Secretary   of   State FOR   THE   ENVIRONMENT,   TRANSPORT   AND   THE REGIONS hereunto affixed is authenticated by—

Richard Jones
Authorised by the Secretary of State

THE COMMON SEAL of THE MOTOR INSURERS' BUREAU was hereunto affixed in the presence of—

James Arthur Read
Roger Merer Jones
Directors of the Board of Management
Byford Louisy
Secretary

NOTES FOR THE GUIDANCE OF VICTIMS OF ROAD TRAFFIC ACCIDENTS

The following notes are for the guidance of anyone who may have a claim on the Motor Insurers' Bureau under this Agreement and their legal advisers. They are not part of the Agreement, their purpose being to deal in ordinary language with the situations which most readily occur. They are not in any way a substitute for reading and applying the terms of this or any other relevant Agreement, nor are they intended to control or influence the legal interpretation of the Agreement. Any enquiries, requests for application forms and general correspondence in connection with the Agreement should be addressed to—

Motor Insurers' Bureau
152 Silbury Boulevard
Central Milton Keynes
Milton Keynes MK9 1NB

Tel: 01908 830001
Fax: 01908 671681
DX: 84753 Milton Keynes 3

1. Introduction — MIB'S role and application of the Agreement

1.1 The role of MIB under this Agreement is to provide a safety net for innocent victims of drivers who have been identified but are uninsured. MIB's funds for this purpose are obtained from levies charged upon insurers and so come from the premiums which are charged by those insurers to members of the public.

1.2 MIB has entered into a series of Agreements with the Secretary of State and his predecessors in office. Under each Agreement MIB undertakes obligations to pay defined compensation in specific circumstances. There are two sets of Agreements, one relating to victims of uninsured drivers (the 'Uninsured Drivers' Agreements) and the other concerned with victims of hit and run or otherwise untraceable drivers (the 'Untraced Drivers' Agreements). These Notes are addressed specifically to the procedures required to take advantage of the rights granted by the Uninsured Drivers Agreements. However, it is not always certain which of the Agreements applies. For guidance in such cases please see the note on Untraced Drivers at paragraph 11 below.

1.3 In order to determine which of the Uninsured Drivers Agreements is applicable to a particular victim's claim, regard must be had to the date of the relevant accident.

This Agreement only applies in respect of claims arising on or after 1st October 1999. Claims arising earlier than that are covered by the following Agreements—

1.3.1 Claims arising in respect of an incident occurring between 1st July 1946 and 28th February 1971 are governed by the Agreement between the Minister of Transport and the Bureau dated 17th June 1946.

1.3.2 Claims arising in respect of an incident occurring between 1st March 1971 and 30th November 1972 are governed by the Agreement between the Secretary of State for the Environment and the Bureau dated 1st February 1971.

1.3.3 Claims arising in respect of an incident occurring between 1st December 1972 and 30th December 1988 are governed by the Agreement between the Secretary of State and the Bureau dated 22nd November 1972.

1.3.4 Claims arising in respect of an incident occurring between 31st December 1988 and 30th September 1999 are governed by the Agreement between the Secretary of State and the Bureau dated 21st December 1988.

2. MIB's obligation

2.1 MIB's basic obligation (see clause 5) is to satisfy judgments which fall within the terms of this Agreement and which, because the Defendant to the proceedings is not insured, are not satisfied.

2.2 This obligation is, however, not absolute. It is subject to certain exceptions where MIB has no liability (see clause 6), there are a number of pre-conditions which the claimant must comply with (see clauses 7 to 15) and there are some limitations on MIB's liability (see clauses 16 and 17).

2.3 MIB does not have to wait for a judgment to be given; it can become party to the proceedings or negotiate and settle the claim if it wishes to do so.

3. Claims which MIB is not obliged to satisfy

MIB is not liable under the Agreement in the case of the following types of claim.

3.1 A claim made in respect of an unsatisfied judgment which does not concern a liability against which Part VI of the Road Traffic Act 1988 requires a vehicle user to insure (see section 145 of the Act). An example would be a case where the accident did not occur in a place specified in the Act. See the definitions of 'unsatisfied judgment' and 'relevant liability' in clause 1.

3.2   A claim in respect of loss or damage caused by the use of a vehicle owned by or in the possession of the Crown (that is the Civil Service, the armed forces and so on) to which Part VI does not apply. If the responsibility for motor insurance has been undertaken by someone else or the vehicle is in fact insured, this exception does not apply. See clause 6(1)(a).

3.3   A claim made against any person who is not required to insure by virtue of section 144 of the Road Traffic Act 1988. See clause 6(1)(b).

3.4   A claim (commonly called subrogated) made in the name of a person suffering damage or injury but which is in fact wholly or partly for the benefit of another who has indemnified, or is liable to indemnify, that person. See clause 6(1)(c).

3.5   A claim in respect of damage to a motor vehicle or losses arising from such damage where the use of the damaged vehicle was itself not covered by a contract of insurance as required by law. See clause 6(1)(d).

3.6   A claim made by a passenger in a vehicle where the loss or damage has been caused by the user of that vehicle if—

3.6.1   the use of the vehicle was not covered by a contract of insurance; and

3.6.2   the claimant knew or could be taken to have known that the vehicle was being used without insurance, had been stolen or unlawfully taken or was being used in connection with crime;

See clause 6(1)(e), (2), (3) and (4).

3.7   A claim in respect of property damage amounting to £300 or less, £300 being the 'specified excess'. See clause 16(2).

3.8   Where the claim is for property damage, the first £300 of the loss and so much of it as exceeds £250,000. See clause 16(3) and (4).

4.   Procedure after the accident and before proceedings

4.1   The claimant must take reasonable steps to establish whether there is in fact any insurance covering the use of the vehicle which caused the injury or damage. First, a claimant has statutory rights under section 154 of the Road Traffic Act 1988 to obtain relevant particulars which he must take steps to exercise even if that involves incurring expense and MIB will insist that he does so. See clause 13(a).

4.2   Other steps will include the following—

4.2.1   The exchange of names, addresses and insurance particulars between those involved either at the scene of the accident or afterwards.

4.2.2   Corresponding with the owner or driver of the vehicle or his representatives. He will be obliged under the terms of his motor policy to inform his insurers and a letter of claim addressed to him will commonly be passed to the insurers who may reply on his behalf. See clause 9(2)(d).

4.2.3   Where only the vehicle's number is known, enquiry of the Driver and Vehicle Licensing Agency at Swansea SA99 1BP as to the registered keeper of the vehicle is desirable so that through him the identity of the owner or driver can be established or confirmed.

4.2.4   Enquiries of the police (see clause 13(b)).

4.3   If enquiries show that there is an insurer who is obliged to accept and does accept the obligation to handle the claim against the user of the vehicle concerned, even though the relevant liability may not be covered by the policy in question, then the claim should be pursued with such insurer.

4.4   If, however, enquiries disclose that there is no insurance covering the use of the vehicle concerned or if the insurer cannot be identified or the insurer asserts that it is under no obligation to handle the claim or if for any other reason it is clear that the insurer will not satisfy any judgment, the claim should be directed to MIB itself.

5.   When proceedings are commenced or contemplated.

5.1   As explained above, MIB does not have to wait for a judgment to be obtained before intervening. Claimants may apply to MIB before the commencement of proceedings. MIB will respond to any claim which complies with clause 7 and must give a reasoned reply to any request for compensation in respect of the claim (see clause 18) although normally a request for compensation will not be met until MIB is satisfied that it is properly based. Interim compensation payments are dealt with at paragraph 8 below.

5.2   It is important that wherever possible claims should be made using MIB's application form, fully completed and accompanied by documents supporting the claim, as soon as possible to avoid unnecessary delays. See clause 7(1). Copies of the form can be obtained on request made by post, telephone, fax or the DX or on personal application to MIB's offices.

5.3   The claimant must give MIB notice *in writing* that he has commenced legal proceedings. The notice, the completed application form (if appropriate) and all necessary documents must be received by MIB no later than 14 days after the date of commencement of proceedings. See clause 9(1) and (2)(a). The date of commencement is determined in accordance with the definitions of 'relevant proceedings' and 'commencement' given in clause 1.

5.4   This notice *must* have with it the following—

5.4.1   a copy of the document originating the proceedings, usually in England and Wales a Claim Form and in Scotland a Sheriff Court Writ or Court of Session Summons (see clause 9(2)(b));

5.4.2   normally the Particulars of Claim endorsed on or served with the Claim Form or Writ (see clause 9(2)(e), although this document may be served later in accordance with clause 9(3) if that applies);

5.4.3   in any case the documents required by the relevant rules of procedure (see clause 9(2)(f)).

5.5   In addition, other items as mentioned in clause 9(2), e.g., correspondence with the Defendant (or Defender) or his representatives, need to be supplied where appropriate.

5.6   It is for the claimant to satisfy himself that the notice has in fact been received by MIB. Clause 8 applies to service of documents by post and fax. MIB prefer service by fax as it is almost instantaneous and can be confirmed quickly. Claimants should note that service of documents by DX is not permitted under the Agreement since delivery cannot be proved.

5.7   It should be noted that when MIB has been given notice of a claim, it may elect to require the claimant to bring proceedings and attempt to secure a judgment against the party whom MIB alleges to be wholly or partly responsible for the loss or damage or who may be contracted to indemnify the claimant.

In such a case MIB must indemnify the claimant against the costs of such proceedings. Subject to that, however, MIB's obligation to satisfy the judgment in the action will only arise if the claimant commences the proceedings and takes all reasonable steps to obtain a judgment. See clause 14(a).

6. Service of proceedings

6.1 If proceedings are commenced in England or Wales the claimant *must* inform MIB of the date of service (see clause 10(1) and (2)).

6.2 If service of the Claim Form is effected by the Court, notice must be given within 7 days from the earliest of the dates listed in clause 10(3)(a)(i) or (ii) or within 14 days from the date mentioned in clause 10(3)(b) (the date of deemed service under the court's rules of procedure). Claimants are advised to take steps to ensure that the court or the defendant's legal representatives inform them of the date of service as soon as possible. Although a longer period is allowed than in other cases, service may be deemed to have occurred without a Claimant knowing of it until some time afterwards.

6.3 Where proceedings are served personally, notice must be given 7 days from the date of personal service (see clause 10(3)(a)(iii)).

6.4 In Scotland, proceedings are commenced at the date of service (see clause 1) so notice should already have been given under clause 9 and clause 10 does not apply there.

7. After service and before judgment

7.1 Notice of the filing of a defence, of an amendment to the Statement or Particulars of Claim, and the setting down of the case for trial must be given not later than 7 days after the occurrence of such events and a copy of the document must be supplied (see clause 11(1)).

7.2 MIB may request further information and documents to support the claim where it is not satisfied that the documents supplied with the application form are sufficient to enable it to assess its liability under the Agreement (see clause 11(2)).

7.3 If the claimant intends to sign or apply for judgment he must give MIB notice of the fact before doing so. This notice must be given at least 35 days before the application is to be made or the date when judgment is to be signed (see clause 12).

7.4 At no time must the claimant oppose MIB if it wishes to be joined as a party to proceedings and he must if requested consent to any application by MIB to be joined. Conflicts may arise between a Defendant and MIB which require MIB to become a Defendant or, in Scotland, a party Minuter if a defence is be filed on its behalf (see clause 14(b)).

8. Interim payments

In substantial cases, the claimant may wish to apply for an interim payment. MIB will consider such applications on a voluntary basis but otherwise the claimant has the right to apply to the court for an interim payment order which, if granted, will be met by MIB.

9. After judgment

9.1 MIB's basic obligation normally arises if a judgment is not satisfied within 7 days after the claimant has become entitled to enforce it (see clause 1). However, that judgement may in certain circumstances be set aside and with it MIB's obligation to satisfy it. Sometimes MIB wishes to apply to set aside a judgment either wholly or partially. If MIB decides not to satisfy a judgment it will notify the claimant as soon as possible. Where a judgment is subsequently set aside, MIB will require the claimant to repay any sum previously paid by MIB to discharge its obligation under the Agreement (see clause 15(b)).

9.2 MIB is not obliged to satisfy a judgment unless the claimant has in return assigned the benefit to MIB or its nominee (see clause 15(a)). If such assignment is effected and if the subject matter of the judgment includes claims in respect of which MIB is not obliged to meet any judgment and if MIB effects any recovery on the judgment, the sum recovered will be divided between MIB and the claimant in proportion to the liabilities which were and which were not covered by MIB's obligation (see clause 21).

10. Permissible deductions from payments by MIB

10.1 Claims for loss and damage for which the claimant has been compensated or indemnified, e.g., under a contract of insurance or under the Policyholders Protection Act 1975, and which has not been taken into account in the judgment, may be deducted from the sum paid in settlement of MIB's obligation (see clause 17).

10.2 If there is a likelihood that the claimant will receive payment from such a source after the judgment has been satisfied by MIB, MIB will require him to undertake to repay any sum which duplicates the compensation assessed by the court (see clause 1 5 (b)).

11. Untraced drivers

11.1 Where the owner or driver of a vehicle cannot be identified application may be made to MIB under the relevant Untraced Drivers Agreement. This provides, subject to specified conditions, for the payment of compensation for personal injury. It does not provide for compensation in respect of damage to property.

11.2 In those cases where it is unclear whether the owner or driver of a vehicle has been correctly identified it is sensible for the claimant to register a claim under both this Agreement and the Untraced Drivers Agreement following which MIB will advise which Agreement will, in its view, apply in the circumstances of the particular case.

Motor Insurers' Bureau (Compensation of Victims of Untraced Drivers) Agreement 1996

Text of an Agreement dated the 14th June 1996 between the Secretary of State for Transport and Motor Insurers' Bureau together with some notes on its scope and purpose

THE AGREEMENT
RECITALS

(1)   On 21 April 1969 the Minister of Transport and Motor Insurers' Bureau entered into an Agreement ('the First Agreement') to secure compensation for third party victims of road accidents when the driver responsible for the accident could not be traced.

(2)   The First Agreement was replaced by a new Agreement ('the Second Agreement') which operated in respect of accidents occurring on or after 1 December 1972.

(3)   The Second Agreement was added to by a Supplemental Agreement dated 7 December 1977 ('the Third Agreement') which operated in respect of accidents occurring on or after 3 January 1978.

(4)   The Second Agreement and the Third Agreement have now been replaced by a new Agreement ('this Agreement') which operates in respect of accidents occurring on or after 1 July 1996.

(5)   The text of this Agreement is as follows—

TEXT OF THE AGREEMENT
AN AGREEMENT made the Fourteenth day of June 1996 between the Secretary of State for Transport ('the Secretary of State') and the Motor Insurers' Bureau

whose registered office is at 152 Silbury Boulevard, Milton Keynes, MK9 1NB ('the MIB.').

IT IS HEREBY AGREED as follows—

1.   (1)   Subject to paragraph (2) of this Clause, this Agreement applies to any case in which an application is made to the MIB for a payment in respect of the death of or bodily injury to any person caused by or arising out of the use of a motor vehicle on a road in Great Britain and the case is one in which the following conditions are fulfilled, that is to say:

(a)   the event giving rise to the death or injury occurred on or after 1 July 1996;

(b)   the applicant for the payment either—

(i)   is unable to trace any person responsible for the death or injury, or

(ii)   in a case to which Clause 5 applies where more than one person was responsible, is unable to trace one of those persons. (Any person so untraced is referred to as 'the untraced person');

(c)   the death or injury was caused in such circumstances that on the balance of probabilities the untraced person would be liable to pay damages to the applicant in respect of the death or injury;

(d)   the liability of the untraced person to pay damages to the applicant is one which is required to be covered by insurance or security under Part VI of the Road Traffic Act 1988 ('the 1988 Act'), it being assumed for this purpose, in the absence of evidence to the contrary, that the vehicle was being used in circumstances in which the user was required by the 1988 Act to be insured or secured against third party risks;

(e)   the death or injury was not caused by the use of the vehicle by the untraced person in any deliberate attempt to cause the death or injury of the person in respect of which an application is made;

(f)   the application is made in writing within three years from the date of the event giving rise to the death or injury; and

(g)   the incident was reported to the police within fourteen days or as soon as the applicant reasonably could and the applicant co-operated with the police.

(2)   This Agreement does not apply to a case in which:

(a)   the death or bodily injury in respect of which any such application is made was caused by or arose out of the use of a motor vehicle which at the time of the event giving rise to the death or bodily injury was owned by or in the possession of the Crown, unless the case is one in which some other person has undertaken responsibility for the existence of a contract of insurance under the 1988 Act;

(b)   at the time of the accident the person suffering death or bodily injury in respect of which the application is made was allowing himself to be carried in a vehicle and either before or after the commencement of his journey in the vehicle, if he could reasonably be expected to have alighted from the vehicle, he knew or had reason to believe that the vehicle—

(i)   had been stolen or unlawfully taken, or

(ii)   was being used without there being in force in relation to its use a contract of insurance which complied with the 1988 Act; or

(iii)   was being used in the course or furtherance of crime; or

(iv)   was being used as a means of escape from or avoidance of lawful apprehension.

(3)   For the purpose of paragraph (2) of this Clause:

(a)   a vehicle which has been unlawfully removed from the possession of the Crown shall be taken to continue in that possession whilst it is kept so removed;

(b)   references to a person being carried in a vehicle include references to his being carried in or upon, or entering or getting on to or alighting from the vehicle;

(c)   'owner' in relation to a vehicle which is the subject of a hiring agreement or a hire purchase agreement means the person in possession of the vehicle under that agreement.

2.   (1)   An application to the MIB for a payment in respect of the death or bodily injury to any person may be made:

(a)   by the person for whose benefit that payment is to be made ('the applicant'); or

(b)   by any solicitor acting for the applicant; or

(c)   by any other person whom the MIB may be prepared to accept as acting for the applicant.

(2)   Any decision made, or award or payment given or other thing done in accordance with this Agreement to or by a person acting under paragraph (1)(b) and (1)(c) of this Clause on behalf of the applicant, or in relation to an application made by such person, shall whatever may be the age, or the circumstances affecting the capacity, of the applicant, be treated as having the same effect as if it had been done to or by, or in relation to an application made by, an applicant of full age and capacity.

3.   Subject to the following provisions of this Agreement, the MIB shall, on any application made to it in a case to which this Agreement applies, award to the applicant in respect of the death or injury for which the application is made a payment of an amount which shall be assessed in like manner as a court applying English law in a case where the event giving rise to the death or injury occurred in England or Wales or applying the law of Scotland in a case where that event occurred in Scotland, would assess the damages which the applicant would have been entitled to recover from the untraced prerson in respect of that death or injury if the applicant had brought successful proceedings to enforce a claim for such damages against the untraced person.

4.   In assessing the level of an award in accordance with Clause 3, the MIB shall be under no obligation to include any sum in respect of loss of earnings suffered by the applicant where and in so far as the applicant has in fact been paid wages or salary or any sum in lieu of the same, whether or not such payments were made subject to an undertaking on the part of the applicant to repay the same in the event of the applicant recovering damages.

5.   (1)   This Clause applies to any case:

(a)   to which this Agreement applies; and

(b)   the death or bodily injury in respect of which an application has been made to the MIB under this Agreement ('the relevant death or injury') was caused—

(i)   partly by the untraced person and partly by an identified person or by identified persons, or

(ii)   partly by the untraced person and partly by some other untraced person or persons whose master or principal can be identified; and

(c)   in circumstances making the identified person or persons or any master or principal ('the identified person') liable to the applicant in respect of the relevant death or injury.

(2)   If in a case to which this Clause applies one of the conditions in paragraph (3) of this Clause is satisfied, the amount of the award to be paid by the MIB to the applicant in respect of the relevant death or injury shall be determined in accordance with paragraph (4) of this Clause and its liability to the applicant shall be subject to paragraph (7) of this Clause and Clause 6 of this Agreement.

(3)   The conditions referred to in paragraph (2) of this Clause are—

(a)   that the applicant has obtained a judgment in respect of the relevant death or injury against the identified person ('the original judgment') which has not been satisfied in full within three months from the date on which the applicant became entitled to enforce it ('the three month period'); or

(b)   that the applicant—

(i)   has not obtained and has not been required by the MIB to obtain a judgment in respect of the relevant death or injury against the identified person; and

(ii)   has not received any payment by way of compensation from the identified person or persons.

(4)   The amount to be awarded by the MIB to the applicant in a case to which this Clause applies shall be determined as follows:

(a)   if the condition in paragraph (3)(a) of this Clause is satisfied and the original judgment is wholly unsatisfied within the three month period, the amount to be awarded shall be an amount equal to that proportion of a full award attributable to the untraced person;

(b)   if the condition in paragraph (3)(a) of this Clause is satisfied but the original judgment is satisfied in part only within the three month period, the amount to be awarded—

(i)   if the unsatisfied part of the original judgment is less than the proportion of a full award attributable to the untraced person, shall be an amount equal to that unsatisfied part; or

(ii)   if the unsatisfied part of the original judgment is equal to or greater than the proportion of a full award attributable to the untraced person, shall be an amount equal to the untraced person's proportion;

(c)   if the condition in paragraph (3)(b) of this Clause is satisfied the amount to be awarded shall be an amount equal to the proportion of a full award attributable to the untraced person.

(5)   The following provisions of this paragraph shall have effect in any case in which an appeal from or any proceeding to set aside the original judgment is commenced within a period of three months beginning on the date on which the applicant became entitled to enforce the original judgment:

(a)   until the appeal or proceeding is disposed of the provisions of this Clause shall have effect as if for the three month period there were substituted a period expiring on the date when the appeal or proceeding is disposed of;

(b)   if as a result of the appeal or proceeding, the applicant ceases to be entitled to receive any payment in respect of the relevant death or injury from any of the person or persons against whom he has obtained the original judgment, the provisions of this Clause shall have effect as if he had neither obtained nor been required by the MIB to obtain a judgment against any person or persons;

(c)   if as a result of the appeal or proceeding, the applicant becomes entitled to recover an amount which differs from that which he was entitled to recover under the original judgment the provisions of this Clause shall have effect as if for the reference in paragraph (3)(a) to the original judgment there were substituted a reference to the judgment under which the applicant became entitled to the different amount;

(d)   if as a result of the appeal or proceeding the applicant remains entitled to enforce the original judgment the provisions of this Clause shall have effect as if for the three month period there were substituted a period of three months beginning on the date on which the appeal or other proceeding was disposed of.

The provisions of this paragraph shall apply also in any case where any judgment given upon any appeal or proceeding is itself the subject of a further appeal or similar proceeding and shall apply in such a case in relation to that further appeal or proceeding in the same manner as they apply in relation to the first mentioned appeal or proceeding.

(6)   In this Clause:

(a)   'full award' means the amount which would have fallen to be awarded to the applicant under Clause 3 in respect of the relevant death or injury if the untraced person had been adjudged by a court to be wholly responsible for that death or injury; and

(b)   'the proportion of a full award attributable to the untraced person' means that proportion of a full award which on the balance of probabilities would have been apportioned by a court in proceedings between the untraced person and any other person liable in respect of the same event as the share to be borne by the untraced person in the responsibility for the event giving rise to the relevant death or injury.

(7)   The MIB shall not be under any liability in respect of the relevant death or injury if the applicant is entitled to receive compensation from the MIB in respect of that death or injury under any agreement providing for the compensation of victims of uninsured drivers entered into between the Secretary of State and the MIB.

6.   (1)   Any liability falling upon the MIB upon an application made to it under this Agreement, in respect of any death or injury, shall be subject to the following conditions:

(a)   the applicant shall give all assistance as may reasonably be required by or on behalf of the MIB to enable any investigation to be carried out under this Agreement, including, in particular the provision of statements and information either in writing, or, if required, orally at an interview or interviews between the applicant and any person acting on behalf of the MIB;

(b)   at any time before the MIB has communicated its decision upon the application to the applicant, the applicant shall, subject to the following provisions of this Clause, take all steps as in the circumstances it is reasonable for the MIB to require him to take to obtain judgment against any person or persons in respect of their liability to the applicant for the death or injury as having caused or contributed to the death or injury or as being the master or principal of any person who has caused or contributed to the death or injury; and

(c)   if required by the MIB the applicant shall assign to the MIB or to its nominee any judgment obtained by him (whether or not obtained in accordance with a requirement under subparagraph (b) of this paragraph) in respect of the death or injury to which his application to the MIB relates upon terms as will secure that the MIB or its nominee shall be accountable to the applicant for any amount by which the aggregate of all sums recovered by the MIB or its nominee under the judgment (after deducting all reasonable expenses incurred in effecting recovery) exceeds the amount payable by the MIB to the applicant under this Agreement in respect of that death or injury.

(2)   If the MIB requires the applicant to bring proceedings against any specified person or persons:

(a)   the MIB shall indemnify the applicant against all costs reasonably incurred by him in complying with that requirement unless the result of those proceedings materially contributes to establishing that the untraced person did not cause or contribute to the relevant death or injury; and

(b)   the applicant shall, if required by the MIB and at its expense, provide the MIB with a transcript of any official shorthand note taken in those proceedings of any evidence given or judgment delivered therein.

(3)   In the event of a dispute arising between the applicant and the MIB as to the reasonableness of any requirement by the MIB under paragraph (1)(b) of this Clause or as to whether any costs as referred to in paragraph (2)(a) of this Clause were reasonably incurred, that dispute shall be referred to the Secretary of State whose decision shall be final. Provided that any dispute arising between the applicant and the MIB as to whether the MIB is required to indemnify him under paragraph (2)(a) of this Clause shall, in so far as it depends on the question whether the result of any proceedings which the MIB has required the applicant to bring against any specified person or persons has or has not materially contributed to establish that the untraced person did not cause or contribute to the relevant death or injury, be referred to the arbitrator in accordance with the following provisions of this Agreement, whose decision on that question shall be final.

7.   The MIB shall cause any application made to it for a payment under this Agreement to be investigated and, unless it decides that the application should be rejected because a preliminary investigation has disclosed that the case is not one to which this Agreement applies, it shall cause a report to be made on the application and on the basis of that report it shall decide whether to make an award and, if so, the amount of the award which shall be calculated in accordance with the provisions of this Agreement.

8.   The MIB may before coming to a decision on any application made to it under this Agreement request the applicant to provide it with a statutory declaration to be made by the applicant, setting out to the best of his knowledge, information and belief the facts and circumstances upon which his claim to an

award under this Agreement are based, or facts and circumstances as may be specified by it.

9.   (1)   The MIB shall notify its decision to the applicant and when so doing shall:

(a)   if the application is rejected because a preliminary investigation has disclosed that it is not one made in a case to which this Agreement applies, give its reasons for the rejection; or

(b)   if the application has been fully investigated provide him with a statement setting out—

(i)   the circumstances in which the death or injury occurred and the relevant evidence;

(ii)   the circumstances relevant to the assessment of the amount to be awarded to the applicant under this Agreement and the relevant evidence; and

(iii)   if it refuses to make an award, its reasons for that refusal; and

(c)   in a case to which Clause 5 of this Agreement applies specify the way in which the amount of that award has been computed and its relation to those provisions of Clause 5 which are relevant to its computation.

(2)   Where the MIB has decided that it will not indemnify the applicant against the costs of any proceedings which it has under Clause 6(1)(b) required him to bring against any specified person or persons on the ground that those proceedings have materially contributed to establish that the untraced person did not cause or contribute to the relevant death or injury, it shall give notice to the applicant of that decision, together with its reasons for it and shall provide the applicant with a copy of any transcript of any evidence given or judgment delivered in those proceedings as is mentioned in Clause 6(2)(b) which it regards as relevant to that decision.

10.   (1)   Subject to the provisions of this Agreement, where the MIB has decided to make an award to the applicant, it shall pay the applicant the amount of that award if:

(a)   it has been notified by the applicant that the award is accepted; or

(b)   at the expiration of the period during which the applicant may give notice of an appeal under Clause 11 the applicant has not given the MIB either any notification of acceptance of its award or a notice of an appeal under Clause 11.

(2)   Such payment as is made under paragraph (1) of this Clause shall discharge the MIB from all liability under this Agreement in respect of the death or injury for which that award has been made.

11.   (1)   The applicant shall have a right of appeal to an arbitrator against any decision notified to him by the MIB under Clause 9 if:

(a)   he gives notice to the MIB, that he wishes to appeal against its decision ('the notice of appeal');

(b)   he gives the MIB the notice of appeal within 6 weeks from the date when he was given notice of the decision against which he wishes to appeal; and

(c)   he has not previously notified the MIB that he has accepted its decision.

(2)   The grounds of appeal are as follows:

(a)   where the application has not been the subject of a full investigation—

(i)   that the case is one to which this Agreement applies; and

(ii)   that the applicant's application should be fully investigated by the MIB with a view to its deciding whether or not to make an award to him and, if so, the amount of that award; or

(b)   where the application has been fully investigated—

(i)   that the MIB was wrong in refusing to make an award; or

(ii)   that the amount it has awarded to the applicant is insufficient; or

(c)   in a case where a decision not to indemnify the applicant against the costs of any proceedings has been notified to the applicant by the MIB under Clause 9(2), that that decision was wrong.

12.   A notice of appeal under Clause 11 shall state the grounds of the appeal and shall be accompanied by an undertaking given by the applicant or by the person acting on his behalf under Clause 2(1)(b) and 2(1)(c), that:

(a)   the applicant will accept the decision of the arbitrator; and

(b)   the arbitrator's fee shall be paid to the MIB by the applicant or by the person who has given the undertaking in any case where the MIB is entitled to reimbursement of that fee under the provisions of Clause 22.

13.   (1)   When giving notice of his appeal or at any time before doing so, the applicant may:

(a)   make comments to the MIB on its decision; and

(b)   supply it with such particulars as he thinks fit of any further evidence not contained in the written statement supplied to him by the MIB which he considers is relevant to the application.

(2)   The MIB may, before submitting the applicant's appeal to the arbitrator:

(a)   cause an investigation to be made into the further evidence supplied by the applicant under paragraph (1)(b) of this Clause; and

(b)   report to the applicant the result of that investigation and of any change in its decision which may result from it.

(3)   The applicant may, within six weeks from the date on which the report referred to in paragraph (2)(b) of this Clause was sent to him, unless he withdraws his appeal, make such comments on the report as he may desire to have submitted to the arbitrator.

14.   (1)   In a case where the MIB receives from the applicant a notice of appeal in which the only ground of appeal which is stated is that the amount awarded to the applicant is insufficient, before submitting that appeal to the arbitrator, the MIB may:

(a)   give notice to the applicant that if the appeal proceeds it will request the arbitrator to decide whether the case is one in which the MIB should make an award at all; and

(b)   at the same time as complying with paragraph (1)(a) of this Clause provide the applicant with a statement setting out such comments as it may consider relevant to the decision which the arbitrator should come to on that question.

(2)   Where the MIB gives the applicant notice under paragraph (1)(a) of this Clause, the applicant may, within six weeks from the date on which that notice is given:

(a)   make comments to the MIB and supply it with particulars of other evidence not contained in any written statement provided to him by the MIB as he may consider relevant to the question which the arbitrator is by that notice requested to decide; and

(b)   Clause 13 shall apply in relation to any comments made or particulars supplied by the applicant under paragraph (2)(a) of this Clause.

15.   (1)   Subject to paragraph (2) of this Clause, where the MIB receives a notice of appeal from the applicant under the provisions of this Agreement, unless the appeal is previously withdrawn, it shall:

(a)   submit that appeal to an arbitrator for a decision; and

(b)   send to the arbitrator for the purpose of obtaining his decision—

(i)   the application made by the applicant;

(ii)   a copy of its decision as notified to the applicant; and

(iii)   copies of all statements, declarations, notices, undertakings, comments, transcripts, particulars of reports provided, given or sent to the MIB under this Agreement either by the applicant or any person acting for him under Clause 2(1)(b) or 2(1)(c) or given or sent to the applicant or a person acting for him under Clause 2(1)(b) or 2(1)(c) by the MIB.

(2)   In a case where the MIB causes an investigation to be made under Clause 13, the MIB shall not comply with paragraph (1) of this Clause until:

(a)   the expiration of six weeks from the date on which it sent the applicant a report as to the result of that investigation; or

(b)   the expiration of six weeks from the date on which it gave the applicant notice under Clause 14(1); or

(c)   the expiration of six weeks from the date on which it sent the applicant a report as to the result of that investigation, if it has caused an investigation to be made into any evidence supplied under Clause 14(2).

16.   On an appeal made by the applicant in accordance with this Agreement:

(a)   if the appeal is against a decision by the MIB rejecting an application because a preliminary investigation has disclosed that the case is not one to which this Agreement applies, the arbitrator shall decide whether the case is or is not one to which this Agreement applies and, if he decides that it is such a case, shall remit the application to the MIB for full investigation and a decision in accordance with the provisions of this Agreement;

(b)   if the appeal is against a decision by the MIB given after an application has been fully investigated by it (whether before the appeal or in consequence of its being remitted for such investigation under paragraph (a) of this Clause) the arbitrator shall decide, as may be appropriate, having regard to the grounds stated in the notice of appeal and to any notice given by the MIB to the applicant under Clause 14, whether the MIB should make an award under this Agreement to the applicant and, if so, the amount which it should award to him under the provisions of this Agreement;

(c)   if the appeal relates to a dispute which has arisen between the applicant and the MIB which is required by the proviso to Clause 6(3) to be referred to the arbitrator, the arbitrator shall also give his decision on that dispute.

Provided that where the arbitrator has allowed an appeal under paragraph (a) of this Clause all the provisions of this Agreement shall apply as if the case were an application to which this Agreement applies upon which the MIB had not communicated a decision.

17. (1) Subject to paragraph (2) of this Clause, the arbitrator shall decide the appeal on the documents submitted to him under Clause 15(1)(b) and no further evidence shall be produced to him.

(2) The following shall apply where documents have been submitted to the arbitrator under Clause 15(1)(b):

(a) the arbitrator shall be entitled to ask the MIB to make any further investigation which he considers desirable and to submit a written report of its findings to him for his consideration; and

(b) the MIB shall send a copy of that report to the applicant who shall be entitled to submit written comments on it to the MIB within four weeks of the date on which that copy is sent to him; and

(c) the MIB shall transmit those comments to the arbitrator for his consideration.

18. The arbitrator by whom an appeal made by an applicant in accordance with the provisions of this Agreement shall be considered shall be an arbitrator to be selected by the Secretary of State from two panels of Queen's Counsel appointed respectively by the Lord Chancellor and the Lord Advocate for the purpose of determining appeals under this Agreement, the arbitrator to be selected from the panel appointed by the Lord Chancellor in cases where the event giving rise to the death or injury occurred in England or Wales and from the panel appointed by the Lord Advocate where that event occurred in Scotland.

19. The arbitrator shall notify his decision on any appeal under this Agreement to the MIB and the MIB shall forthwith send a copy of the arbitrator's decision to the applicant.

20. Subject to the provisions of this Agreement, the MIB shall pay the applicant any amount which the arbitrator has decided shall be awarded to him, and that payment shall discharge the MIB from all liability under this Agreement in respect of the death or injury in respect of which that decision has been given.

21. Each party to the appeal will bear their own costs.

22. The MIB shall pay the arbitrator a fee approved by the Lord Chancellor or the Lord Advocate, as the case may be, after consultation with the MIB.

Provided that, in any case where it appears to the arbitrator, that there were no reasonable grounds for the appeal, the arbitrator may in his discretion decide:

(a) that his fee ought to be paid by the applicant; and

(b) that the person giving the undertaking required by Clause 12 shall be liable to reimburse the MIB the amount of the fee paid by it to the arbitrator, except in so far as that amount is deducted by the MIB from any amount which it is liable to pay to the applicant in consequence of the decision of the arbitrator.

23. If in any case it appears to the MIB that by reason of the applicant being under the age of majority or of any other circumstances affecting his capacity to manage his affairs it would be in the applicant's interest that all or some part of the amount which would otherwise be payable to him under an award made under this Agreement should be administered for him by the Family Welfare Association or by some other body or person under a trust or by the Court of Protection (or in Scotland by the appointment of a Judicial Factor) the MIB may establish for that purpose a trust of the whole or part of the amount to take effect for a period and under provisions as may appear to it to be appropriate in the

circumstances of the case or may initiate or cause any other person to initiate process in that Court and otherwise cause any amount payable under the award to be paid to and administered thereby.

24.   In any case in which an application has been made to the MIB under Clause 2(1) and in which a preliminary investigation under Clause 7 has disclosed that the case is one to which the Agreement, save for Clause 5, applies, the MIB may, instead of causing a report to be made on the application as provided by Clause 7, make, or cause to be made, to the applicant an offer to settle his application in a specified sum, assessed in accordance with Clause 3.

25.   Where an offer is made under Clause 24, there shall be provided to the applicant (at the same time) in writing particulars of:

(a)   the circumstances in which the death or injury occurred and the relevant evidence; and

(b)   the circumstances relevant to the assessment of the amount to be awarded to the applicant and the relevant evidence.

26.   (1)   On receipt by the MIB or its agent of an acceptance of the offer referred to in Clause 24:

(a)   this acceptance shall have effect in relation to the application as if in Clause 7 the words 'and, unless the MIB decides' to the end of the Clause, and Clauses 9 to 22 inclusive were omitted; and

(b)   the MIB shall pay to the applicant the amount specified in the offer.

(2)   The payment made by the MIB under paragraph (1)(b) of this Clause shall discharge it from all liability under this Agreement in respect of the death or injury for which the payment has been made.

27.   This Agreement may be determined at any time by the Secretary of State or by the MIB by either of them giving to the other no less than twelve months previous notice in writing. Provided that this Agreement shall continue to have effect in any case where the event giving rise to the death or injury occurred before the date on which this Agreement terminates in accordance with any notice so given.

28.   From 14 June 1996 the following periods of operation shall apply:

(a)   this Agreement shall come into operation on 1 July 1996 in relation to accidents occurring on or after that date;

(b)   the Second Agreement shall cease and determine except in relation to applications arising out of accidents which occurred on or after 1 December 1972 and before the 1 July 1996; and

(c)   the Third Agreement shall cease and determine except in relation to accidents occurring on or after 3 January 1978 and before the 1 July 1996.

IN WITNESS whereof the Secretary of State for Transport has caused his Corporate Seal to be hereto affixed and the Motor Insurers' Bureau has caused its Common Seal to be hereto affixed the day and year first above written.

THE CORPORATE SEAL of THE SECRETARY OF STATE FOR TRANSPORT hereunto affixed is authenticated by:
Steven Norris
Parliamentary Under Secretary of State
Department of Transport

THE COMMON SEAL of THE MOTOR INSURERS' BUREAU was hereunto affixed in the presence of:
James A Read
Leslie Howell
Directors of the Board of Management

Anthony Dand
Secretary

NOTES

The following Notes are for the guidance of those who may wish to make application to the Motor Insurers' Bureau for payment under the Agreement, and for the guidance of their legal advisers, but they must not be taken as making unnecessary a careful study of the Agreement itself. Communications connected with the Agreement should be addressed to the Motor Insurers' Bureau ('the MIB'), whose address is 152 Silbury Boulevard, Central Milton Keynes, MK9 1NB.

1.   This Agreement replaces a previous one dated 22 November 1972 and a Supplemental Agreement dated 7 December 1977 and continues the arrangements which have existed since 1946 under which the MIB has made ex gratia payments in respect of death or personal injuries resulting from the use on the road of a motor vehicle the owner or driver of which cannot be traced. Provision is made for an appeal against the MIB's decision in such cases.
2.   The Agreement dated 22 November 1972 applies to a death or bodily injury arising out of an accident occurring on a road in Great Britain on or after 1 December 1972 and before 3 January 1978. The Agreement dated 22 November 1972 as supplemented by the Supplemental Agreement dated 7 December 1977 applies in relation to accidents occurring on or after 3 January 1978 and before 1 July 1996. This Agreement applies in relation to accidents occurring on or after 1 July 1996.
3.   Subject to the terms of the Agreement, the MIB will accept applications for a payment in respect of the death of, or bodily injury to any person resulting from the use of a motor vehicle on a road in Great Britain in any cases in which:

(a)   the applicant for the payment cannot trace any person responsible for the death or injury (or, in certain circumstances, a person partly responsible) (Clause 1(1)(b)); and

(b)   the death or injury was caused in such circumstances that the untraced person would be liable to pay damages to the applicant in respect of the death or injury (Clause 1(1)(d)).

(c)   the untraced person's liability to the applicant is one which at the time the accident occurred, was required to be covered by insurance or security (Clause 1(1)(d)).

The MIB will not deal with the following:

(a)   deliberate 'running down' cases (Clause 1(1)(e));

(b)   certain other cases relating to Crown vehicles; and

(c)   certain categories of 'voluntary' passenger (Clause 1(2)–(4)).

4.   Applications for a payment under the Agreement must be made in writing to the MIB within 3 years of the date of the accident giving rise to the death or injury (Clause 1(1)(f)).

5.   Under Clause 3, the amount which the MIB will award will (except for the exclusion of those elements of damages mentioned in Clause 4 be assessed in the same way as a Court would have assessed the amount of damages payable by the untraced person had the applicant been able to bring a successful claim for damages against him.

6.   Clause 5 relates to cases where an untraced person, and identified person are partly responsible for a death or injury, and defines the conditions under which the MIB will in such cases make a contribution in respect of the responsibility of the untraced person.

7.   Under Clause 6(1)(b), the MIB may require the applicant to bring proceedings against any identified person who may be responsible for the death or injury, subject to indemnifying the applicant as to his costs as provided in Clause 6(2) and (3).

8.   On receipt of an application, the MIB will, if satisfied that the application comes within the terms of the Agreement, investigate the circumstances and, when this has been done, decide whether to make a payment and, if so, how much (Clause 7).

9.   The MIB may request the applicant to make a statutory declaration setting out all, or some, of the facts on which his application is based (Clause 8).

10.   The MIB may notify the applicant of its decision, setting out the circumstances of the case and the evidence on which it bases its decision, and, if it refuses to make a payment, the reasons for the refusal (Clause 9).

11.   If the applicant wishes to appeal against the decision on the grounds specified in Clause 11(2), he must notify the MIB within six weeks of being notified of the decision, and he or any person acting on his behalf shall give the undertakings set out in Clause 12.

12.   The MIB may, as a result of the comments made and further evidence submitted by the applicant on its decision, investigate the further evidence, and if so it will communicate with the applicant again. In such a case the applicant will have six weeks from the date of that further communication in which to decide whether or not to go on with the appeal (Clause 13).

13.   Where the applicant appeals only on the ground that the amount awarded to him is too low, the MIB may give him notice that if the matter proceeds to appeal, it will ask the arbitrator to decide also the issue of the MIB's liability to make any payment. The applicant will have six weeks from the date of any such notice in which to comment to the MIB on this intention (Clause 14).

14.   Appeals will be decided by an arbitrator who will be a Queen's Counsel selected by the Secretary of State for Transport from one of two panels to be appointed by the Lord Chancellor and the Lord Advocate respectively (Clause 18).

15.   All appeals will be decided by the arbitrator on the basis of the relevant documents (as set out in Clause 15) which will be sent to him by the MIB. If the arbitrator asks the MIB to make a further investigation, the applicant will have an opportunity to comment on the result of that investigation (Clause 17).

16.   The arbitrator may, at his discretion, award the cost of his fee against the applicant if he considers the appeal unreasonable; otherwise, each party to the appeal will bear their own costs, the MIB paying the arbitrator's fee (Clause 21 and 22).

17.   In certain circumstances, the MIB may establish a trust for the benefit of an applicant of the whole or part of any award (Clause 23).

Motor Insurers' Bureau Compensation of Victims of Uninsured Drivers (Claim Form)

NOTES FOR THE ASSISTANCE OF CLAIMANTS

The following notes appear in question and answer format and attempt to deal with the questions that are most commonly asked, as well as explaining what the claimant may expect and what is required by MIB. However, these notes do not replace or modify the Agreements and claimants are recommended to read the Agreement under which they are claiming carefully.

Q What is the Motor Insurers' Bureau?
A   The Motor Insurers' Bureau (MIB) is an independent organisation created by the insurance industry to co-operate with the Government in compensating the victims of negligent uninsured motorists.

Q How is MIB financed?
A   Funds sufficient to pay claims are provided by all Motor Insurers in proportion to their market share. Those funds come from the premiums collected from honest motorists.

Q What is the 'Uninsured Drivers' Agreement'?
A   This is an Agreement between the Secretary of State for the Environment, Transport and the Regions and MIB which sets out the circumstances under which claims will be paid. Whilst the Agreement requires that a judgment be obtained in a Civil Court against the uninsured motorist, MIB will, wherever possible, pay compensation by agreement as opposed to demanding that a judgment be obtained first. A copy of the Agreement can be obtained from Her Majesty's Stationery Office or large bookstores for a small fee.

Q When should I claim on MIB?
A   As soon as it becomes clear that the motorist who has caused the injury or damage is uninsured. MIB expects that a claimant will have made common sense enquiries to identify an insurer, which enqiuries will include but not necessarily be limited to:
   (a)   Contacting the motorist.
   (b)   Enquiring of the Driver and Vehicle Licensing Authority in Swansea as to the identify of the registered keeper of the vehicle.
   (c)   Searching any computer database that may be available for the purpose.
   (d)   Making a formal complaint to the police under Section 154 of the Road Traffic Act 1988. (Section 154 makes it an offence for a person against whom a claim is made to withhold details of insurers).

Q What information and/or documents should I provide when returning this form?

A Copies of all correspondence with the motorist, the owner of the vehicle, the motorist's employer or anyone acting on their behalf, including any insurer regardless of whether the insurer denies issuing cover. Your claim will have to be proved so much time can be saved by enclosing documents supporting your claim. For example, estimates for any repair required, or if you have lost earnings, a letter from your employers confirming exactly what has been lost. It is essential that, if you were driving a motor vehicle, you enclose evidence that you were insured at the time, as the Agreement excludes any benefit to uninsured motorists. It is very important that as much information as possible is given, since if information is withheld unreasonably, any Court which hears the case subsequently has the power to impose financial penalties.

Q What will happen after I return the completed form?

A MIB will confirm receipt within 21 days and explain what action is being taken, which action will vary depending on the case and the information you have been able to supply. However, as well as investigating the amount of your claim, we must try and contact the uninsured motorist to obtain his account of the accident as well as his permission to intervene.

Q Why do you need the permission of the uninsured motorist to deal with my claim?

A Even uninsured motorists have the right in law to deal with their own affairs, and the Agreement does not permit us to ignore his rights. However, if the uninsured motorist does not co-operate, we will tell you what options appear to be available to progress your claim.

Q What if the motorist cannot be identified?

A If your claim is for damage to property, then unfortunately we will be unable to help you, as there is no possibility of your obtaining a judgment against the person responsible. However, if you have been injured, you will be able to submit a claim for that injury (but not damage to property) under the Untraced Drivers Agreement, which provides for victims of 'hit and run' accidents.

Q How long will my claim take?

A This is difficult to predict as many different factors are involved.

If your claim is limited to property damage or minor injury it should be resolved in 4 or 5 months, or less.

If, on the other hand, your claim involves contested liability, evidentiary difficulties, or serious injury it may require the police report to be obtained, which can take some time, especially if its release is delayed by criminal prosecutions.

Injury claims can also be delayed if it is difficult for your doctors to agree on the effects, and you may be advised to wait until you have recovered fully, before agreeing any compensation.

MIB will make every effort to reach a decision on responsibility for the accident within three months and to keep you informed. Where there seems to be the prospect of a long delay, MIB will consider an interim payment.

Q Will my claim be paid in full?

A Responsibility for the accident has to be agreed, or decided by a Court, on the evidence, and your claim may be reduced by a proportion, or possibly rejected if the evidence is that you were wholly or partly responsible.

Where MIB accepts a claim is one for payment in full, property damage claims (which include claims for losses stemming from damage to property) will have an excess of £300 deducted.

Injury claims including loss of earnings, are subject to a legal obligation on MIB to refund to the Department of Social Security certain benefits that you have been paid as a result of the accident, and to deduct that amount from your claim for loss of earnings. You are advised by the DSS as to the amount MIB has to pay and if you disagree, you have a right of appeal to the DSS.

Q What can I do if I think I have grounds for complaint?

A MIB deals with all claims in accordance with service standards, and seeks to provide a reasoned response wherever necessary. Nonetheless, if you are dissatisfied, this is what you should do:

(a) Contact your solicitors or representative and ask him to resolve the problem by telephone.

(b) If you are not represented, telephone MIB's Agent and speak to the person handling the claim. If you are not satisfied, write for 'the attention of the Claims Manager'. In the event you feel that the complaint has not been resolved, write to the Claims Manager, MIB, 152 Silbury Boulevard, Central Milton Keynes MK9 1NB, marking the envelope 'Private and Confidential'.

(c) The Chief Executive of MIB is always prepared to review decisions on complaints. Should you wish to do so, please write to him at the same address.

(d) In the event that your problem involves a matter of principle, which may be of public interest and you consider that it has not been dealt with adequately under the above procedure, it is open to you to write to the Minister for Roads and Traffic at the Department of the Environment, Transport and the Regions, Great Minster House, 76 Marsham Street, London SW1P 4DR. The Minister will normally require to be satisfied that the above procedure has been followed before he will intervene.

Important Note: A problem arising from the interpretation of the Agreement can only be resolved by reference to the Court, unless the Agreement specifically empowers the Minister to intervene.

A. DETAILS OF CLAIMANT   Accident Ref:

Title: Mr/Mrs/Miss* First Names:	Surname:
Address:	
Town:	
County:	Postcode:

Status: (delete those inapplicable) Vehicle owner/Driver/Passenger/Pedestrian/Cyclist*	Occupation:	VAT Registered? Y/N VAT Reg. No:
Date of Birth: / /	Telephone No. Home:	Business:

B. DETAILS OF DRIVER OF YOUR VEHICLE AT TIME OF ACCIDENT (or person in charge of vehicle)

Title: Mr/Mrs/Miss* First Names:	Surname:
Address:	
Town:	
County:	Postcode:

Occupation:	Date of Birth:	Telephone No:	VAT Registered?	VAT Reg. No:
	/ /	Home: Business:	Y/N*	

C. DETAILS OF YOUR VEHICLE AND INSURERS

Make:	Model:
Est/Value:	Price Paid & Date:	Year of Registration:

Registration Number:	If vehicle insured please supply identity of:
Is the vehicle owned by you: Y/N*	Insurers (not Broker):
If no, who is the owner:	Address:
Address:	
	Policy Cover, eg. Comp/TPF&T/TP*
Details of damage your vehicle sustained in this accident (please attach estimates from two repairers unless the car is undrivable, when one estimate will be sufficient)	Is claim being made on your Insurer: Y/N*
	Policy No./Reference of Insurers:
	If any other insurers, for example Legal Expense Insurers are involved in your claim, or any other organisation is responsible for your legal expenses, please enter:
Address where vehicle can be inspected and time:	Insurer/Organisation:
	Address:
	Policy/Contract No:
	Show area damaged:
Is vehicle in use? Y/N*	
Have you obtained a replacement: Y/N*	
If yes, Make:	
Model:	
Have you hired a vehicle: Y/N*	
If yes, Make:	
Model:	

D. DAMAGE TO YOUR PROPERTY (if not a motor vehicle)

Type of property:		
Address of Location:		
Town:	County:	Postcode:
Description of Damage:		
Estimate of cost of repair (please attach two estimates):		
Is damage covered by insurance? Y/N* If yes, complete section below:		
Insurers Name:	Policy No./Reference of Insurers:	
Address:		

E. PERSONAL INJURY OF CLAIMANT

Name of Injured Person: Title (Mr/Mrs/Miss): First Name:	Surname:
Hospital:	Telephone No:
Address:	Name and Address of GP:
Town:	
Postcode:	
Brief details of injury:	Name & Address of Employer:

Are you claiming any benefit or losses from any organisation other than MIB? Y/N*

If yes, please set out the nature of the benefits claimed and the name and address and reference numbers of those against whom you are claiming:

Nature of benefit or loss:	Reference No:
Name and address	
Period off work: From: To:	National Insurance No:
Driver/Passenger/Pedestrian/Pedal Cyclist* (*delete where necessary)	Reg. No. of vehicle in which travelling:

F. PERSONAL INJURY OF SECOND CLAIMANT

Name of Injured Person: Title (Mr/Mrs/Miss): First Name:	Surname:
Hospital:	Telephone No:
Address:	Name and Address of GP:
Town:	
Postcode:	
Brief details of injury:	Name & Address of Employer:

Are you claiming any benefit or losses from any organisation other than MIB? Y/N*

If yes, please set out the nature of the benefits claimed and the name and address and reference numbers of those against whom you are claiming:

Nature of benefit or loss:	Reference No:
Name and address	
Period off work: From: To:	National Insurance No:
Driver/Passenger/Pedestrian/Pedal Cyclist* (*delete where necessary)	Reg. No. of vehicle in which travelling:

G. DETAILS OF UNINSURED VEHICLE INVOLVED

Reg No:	Colour:	Name of Driver: Title: Mr/Mrs/Miss First Names: Surname:
Make & Model:		
Description of Driver:		Address:
		Town:
		County: Post code:
Indicate Age of Driver:		Telephone No. Home: Business:
Under 15/Under 20/21-30/31-40/41-50/51-60/61-70/Over 70*		Area of impact
Name of Owner: Title: Mr/Mrs/Miss* First names: Surname:		
Address:		
Town:		
County: Postcode		
Telephone No. Home: Business:		

H. ENQUIRIES WITH UNINSURED MOTORIST

Please specify what enquiries you have made to identify the insurers of the uninsured motorist:

Letter/phone call to motorist YES/NO - If yes, please enclose a copy of the correspondence or the event of a phone call details of any reply:

Enquiry with D.V.L.A. YES/NO - If yes, please enclose D.V.L.A. response.

Enquiry with vehicle owner YES/NO - If yes, please enclose a copy of the response.

Enquiry with possible insurers YES/NO - If yes, please enclose copies of the correspondence.

Name & Address of any Insurers/Brokers mentioned:

Town: County: Postcode: Policy/Reference No:

I. OTHER VEHICLES INVOLVED

Reg No:		Make & Model: .	
Name of Driver:		Name of Owner:	
Title (Mr/Mrs/Miss) First Name: Surname:		Title (Mr/Mrs/Miss) First Name: Surname:	
Address:		Address:	
Town:		Town:	
County: Postcode:		County: Postcode:	
Tel No. Home: Business:		Tel No. Home: Business:	
Area of Impact:			
Name & Address of Insurers/Brokers:			
Town:		County:	
Postcode: Policy/Reference No:			

J. DETAILS OF ACCIDENT

Location:	Street:		Date and time	
	Town:		of accident:	
	County:			

Was accident reported to Police: Y/N | Reference and name of Reporting Officer:

Address of Police Station where reported:

| Town: | County: | Postcode: |

K. DESCRIPTION OF ACCIDENT

L. RESPONSIBILITY (who do you consider to blame and why?)

M. SKETCH OF SCENE (please indicate direction of vehicle(s), road markings etc.)

N. WITNESSES

Title (Mr/Mrs/Miss)	First Name:	Surname:		Title (Mr/Mrs/Miss)	First Name:	Surname
Address:				Address:		
Town:				Town:		
County:	Postcode:			County:		Postcode:
Tel No. Home:	Business:			Tel No. Home:		Business:
Title (Mr/Mrs/Miss)	First Name: Surname:			Title (Mr/Mrs/Miss)	First Name:	Surname
Address:				Address:		
Town:				Town:		
County:	Postcode:			County:		Postcode:
Tel No. Home:	Business:			Tel No. Home:		Business:

O. DECLARATION BY YOU AND THE DRIVER

I/We declare that the replies and information above are true and I/we authorise Motor Insurers' Bureau to make any application on my/our behalf in accordance with the provisions of Section 154 of the Road Traffic Act 1988 or Article 96 of the Road Traffic Act (Northern Ireland) Order 1981 for Northern Ireland.

Signed: _____ Dated: _____
          (Vehicle Owner)

Signed: _____ Dated: _____
          (Driver)

N.B. If there is insufficient space on this form, please attach an additional sheet.

FOR OFFICE USE ONLY				
Handler: _____				Diary Date: _____
Reserve:	PI	PD	Class	DVLA Check Reg: _____
Claimant 1:	_____	_____	_____	MIAFTR? Y/N
Claimant 2:	_____	_____	_____	Other: _____
Claimant 3:	_____	_____	_____	

Index